Japanese
Picture Dictionary

Japanese
Picture Dictionary

Berlitz Publishing/APA Publications GmbH & Co. Verlag KG
Singapore Branch, Singapore

Contacting the Editors
Every effort has been made to provide accurate information in this publication, but changes are inevitable. The publisher cannot be responsible for any resulting loss, inconvenience or injury. We would appreciate it if readers would call our attention to any errors or outdated information by contacting Apa Publications, 38 Joo Koon Road, Singapore 628990. Fax: (65) 6861 6438, E-mail: susan@apasin.com.sg

Cover illustration by Chris L. Demarest
Interior illustrations by Chris L. Demarest (pages 3, 5, 7-9, 12-23, 26-43, 46-51, 54-67, 70-75, 78-85, 88-107, and 110-119)
Anna DiVito (pages 24, 25, 52, 53, 76, 77, 86, 87, and 120-123)
Claude Martinot (pages 10, 11, 44, 45, 68, 69, 108, and 109)

Printed in Singapore

Dear Parents,

The Berlitz Kids™ *Picture Dictionary* will create hours of fun and productive learning for you and your child. Children love sharing books with adults, and reading together is a natural way for your child to develop second-language skills in an enjoyable and entertaining way.

In 1878, Professor Maximilian Berlitz had a revolutionary idea about making language learning accessible and fun. These same principles are still successfully at work today. Now, more than a century later, people all over the world recognize and appreciate his innovative approach. Berlitz Kids™ combines the time-honored traditions of Professor Berlitz with current research to create superior products that truly help children learn foreign languages.

Berlitz Kids™ materials let your child gain access to a second language in a positive way. The content and vocabulary in this book have been carefully chosen by language experts to provide basic words and phrases that form the foundation of a core vocabulary. In addition, the book will delight your child, since each word is used in an amusing sentence in both languages, and then illustrated in an engaging style. The pictures are a great way to capture your child's attention!

You will notice that most words are listed as separate entries. Every so often, though, there is a special page that shows words grouped together by theme. For example, if your child is especially interested in animals, he or she will find a special Animals page with lots of words and pictures grouped there—in both English and the foreign language. In addition, to help your child with phrases used in basic conversation, you and your child may want to look at the back of the book, where phrases about such things as meeting new people and a family dinner can be found.

The Berlitz Kids™ *Picture Dictionary* has an easy-to-use index at the back of the book. This index lists the English words in alphabetical order and gives the page number where the word appears in the main part of the book.

We hope the Berlitz Kids™ *Picture Dictionary* will provide you and your child with hours of enjoyable learning.

The Editors at Berlitz Kids™

a/an
ひとつ hitotsu

A sandwich and an apple are the cat's lunch.

サンドウイッチひとつとりんご
ひとつがそのねこのランチです。
sandouitch hitotsu to ringo hitotsu
ga sono neko no lanchi desu

across
むこうがわに mukoogawani

The fork is across from the spoon.

そのフォークはそのスプーン
のむこうがわにあります。
sono fooku wa sono supuun no
mukoogawa ni arimasu

to add
たす tasu

I like to add numbers.

わたしはかずをたすのが
すきです。
watashi wa kazu o tasunoga
sukidesu

adventure
ぼうけん booken

What an adventure!

なんというぼうけんだ!
nan to iu booken da!

afraid
こわがって kowagatte

The elephant is afraid.

そのぞうはこわがっています。
sono zoo wa kowagatte imasu

after
あとに ato-ni

She eats an apple after lunch.

かのじょはランチのあとにりん
ごをひとつたべます。
kanojo wa lanchi no ato ni ringo
o hitotsu tabemasu

again
くりかえし kurikaeshi

She jumps again and again.

かのじょはくりかえしくりかえし
とびます。
kanojo wa kurikaeshi kurikaeshi
tobimasu

to agree
どういする dooi-suru

They need to agree.

かれらはどういするひつようが
あります。
karera wa dooi-suru hitsuyoo ga
arimasu

air
くうき kuuki

A balloon is full of air.

ふうせんにはくうきがい
っぱいつまっています。
fusen niwa kuuki ga ippai
tsumatte imasu

airplane *See Transportation (page 108).*
ひこうき **hikooki**

airport
くうこう **kuukoo**

Airplanes land at the airport.

ひこうきはそのくうこうに
ちゃくりくします。
hikooki wa sono kuukoo ni
chakuriku shimasu

all
すべて **subete**

All the frogs are green.

すべてのかえるたち
はみどりいろです。
subete no kaeru-tachi
wa midoriiro desu

alligator *See Animals (page 10).*
わに **wani**

almost
もうすこしで
moosukoshi de

He can almost reach it.

かれはもうすこしで
それにとどくことがで
きます。
kare wa moosukoshi de
sore ni todoku koto ga
dekimasu

along
にそって **ni-sotte**

There are birds along the path.

こみちにそってとりたち
がいます。
komichi ni sotte toritachi
ga imasu

already
すでに **sudeni**

He already has a hat.

かれはすでにぼうし
をもっています。
kare wa sudeni booshi
o motteimasu

and
それに **soreni**

I have two sisters and two brothers.

わたしにはふたりのあね
とふたりのあにがいます。
watashi niwa futari no ane
to futari no ani ga imasu

to answer
こたえる **kotaeru**

Who wants to answer the question?

だれがそのしつもんにこ
たえたいのですか?
dare ga sono sitsumon ni
kotaetai no desuka?

ant
See Insects (page 52).
あり ari

apartment
アパート apaato

He is in the apartment.

かれはアパートのなかに
います。
kare wa apaato no naka ni
imasu

apple
りんご ringo

The apple is falling.

そのりんごはおちています。
sono ringo wa ochite imasu

April
しがつ shigatsu

The month after
March is April.

さんがつのつぎのつきは
しがつです。
sangatsu no tugi no tuki wa
shigatsu desu

arm
See People (page 76).
うで ude

armadillo
アルマジロ arumajiro

Some armadillos live
in Mexico.

なんびきかのアルマジロが
メキシコにすんでいます。
nanbiki kano arumajiro ga mekishiko ni sunde imasu

around
まわりを mawari-o

Someone is walking around
the stool.

だれかがまるいすのまわりをあ
るいています。
darekaga maruisu no mawari-o
aruite imasu

art
げいじゅつ geijutsu

Is it art?

それはげいじゅつで
すか?
sore wa geijutsu desuka?

as
とおなじほど
to-onajihodo

He is as tall as a tree!

かれはきとおなじほどせがた
かい!
kare wa ki to-onajihodo se
ga takai!

Animals
どうぶつたち
doobutsu-tachi

kangaroo
カンガルー
kangaruu

monkey
さる
saru

lion
ライオン
laion

elephant
ぞう
zoo

bear
くま
kuma

giraffe
キリン
kirin

jaguar
ヒョウ
hyoo

llama
ラマ
lama

alligator
ワニ
wani

snake
へび
hebi

fox
きつね
kitsune

hippopotamus
ヒポポタマス
hipopotamasu

cow
めうし
meushi

horse
うま
uma

rooster
オンドリ
ondori

rabbit
うさぎ
usagi

goat
やぎ
yagi

sheep
ひつじ
hitsuji

chicken
にわとり
niwatori

pig
ぶた
buta

fish
さかな
usagi

duck
アヒル
ahiru

frog
かえる
kaeru

11

to ask
たずねる tazuneru

It is time to ask,
"Where are my sheep?"

「どこにわたしのひつじが
いるの？」ときくときです。
"doko ni watashi no hitsuji ga
iruno?" to kiku toki desu

at
に ni

The cat is at home.

そのねこはいえにいます。
sono neko wa ie ni imasu

attic *See Rooms in a House (page 86).*
やねうら yaneura

August
はちがつ hachigatsu

The month after July is
August.

しちがつのつぎのつきは
はちがつです。
shichigatsu no tugi no tuki
wa hachigatsu desu

aunt
おば oba

My aunt is my mom's sister.

わたしのおばはわたしの
おかあさんのあねです。
watashi no oba wa watashi no
okaasan no ane desu

awake
めがさめています
me ga samete imasu

The duck is awake.

そのあひるはめがさめ
ています。
sono ahiru wa me ga samete
imasu

away
さってしまう
satte shimau

The cat is going away.

そのねこはさって
しまおうとしています。
sono neko wa satte
shimaou to shite imasu

baby
あかちゃん akachan

The baby likes to eat bananas.

そのあかちゃんはバナナ
をたべるのがすきです。
sono akachan wa banana
o taberu noga sukidesu

back
せなか senaka

She is scratching his back.

かのじょはかれのせなかを
ひっかいています。
kanojo wa kare no senaka o
hikkaite imasu

bad
わるい warui

What a bad, bad monster!

なんてわるい、わるいかいぶ
つだ!
nante warui warui kaibutsu da!

bag
ふくろ fukuro

The bag is full.

そのふくろはいっぱいです。
sono fukuro wa ippai desu

bakery
パンやさん panyasan

Everything at the bakery
smells great!

そのパンやさんではすべてが
いいにおいがします!
sono panyasan dewa subete ga
ii nioi ga shimasu!

ball
ボール boolu

Can he catch the
ball?

かれはそのボールをとら
えることができますか?
kare wa sono boolu o
toraerukoto ga dekimasuka?

balloon
ふうせん fuusen

It is a balloon!

それはふうせんです!
sore wa fuusen desu!

banana
バナナ banana

The bananas are in
the bowl.

そのバナナはそのはちの
なかにあります。
sono banana wa sono hachi no
naka ni arimasu

band
がくだん gakudan

The band is loud.

そのがくだんはさわ
がしい。
sono gakudan wa sawagashii

bandage
ほうたい houtai

She has a bandage on her knee.

かのじょはひざにほうたい
をまいています。
kanojo wa hiza ni houtai o
maite imasu

piggy bank
ちょきんばこ chokin-bako

Put your money
into the piggy bank!

あなたのおかねをちょき
んばこにいれてください!

anata no okane wo chokin-bako
ni irete kudasai!

barber
とこやさん tokoya-san

The barber cuts my hair.

そのとこやさんがわたしの
かみをかります。

sono tokoya-san ga watashi no
kami o karimasu

to bark
ほえる hoeru

Dogs like to bark.

いぬはほえるのがすきです。

inu wa hoeru noga sukidesu

baseball *See Games and Sports (page 44).*
やきゅう yakyuu

basement *See Rooms in a House (page 86).*
ちかしつ chikashitsu

basket
かご kago

What is in the basket?

そのかごのなかにはなに
がありますか?

sono kago no nakaniwa nani
ga arimasuka?

basketball *See Games and Sports (page 44).*
やきゅう yakyuu

bat
こうもり koomori

The bat is sleeping.

そのこうもりはねむっています。

sono koomori wa nemutte imasu

bat
バット batto

Hit the ball with the bat!

そのバットでそのボールを
うちなさい!

sono batto de sono boolu o
uchinasai!

bath
おふろ ofuro

She is taking a bath.

かのじょはおふろにはいって
います。

kanojo wa ofuro ni haitte imasu

bathroom *See Rooms in a House (page 86).*
ふろば furoba

to be
になる ni naru

Would you like to be my friend?

あなたはわたしのともだちに
なりたいですか?

anata wa watashi no tomodachi
ni naritai desuka?

beach
はまべ hamabe

I like to play at the beach.

わたしははまべであそぶの
がすきです。
watashi wa hamabe de asobu
noga sukidesu

beans
まめ mame

He likes to eat beans.

かれはまめをたべるのが
すきです。
kare wa mame o taberu noga
sukidesu

bear See Animals (page 10).
くま kuma

beautiful
うつくしい utukushii

Look at the beautiful things.

うつくしいものをみなさい。
utukushii mono o minasai

because
ので node

She is wet because it is raining.

あめがふっているのでかのじょ
はぬれています。
ame ga futte iru node kanojo
wa nurete imasu

bed
ベッド beddo

The bed is next to the table.

そのベッドはそのテーブルの
なりにあります。
sono beddo wa sono teeburu no
tonari ni arimasu

bedroom See Rooms in a House (page 86).
しんしつ shinshitsu

bee See Insects (page 52).
はち hachii

beetle See Insects (page 52).
カブトムシ kabutomushi

before
まえに maeni

Put on your socks before
you put on your shoes.

くつをはくまえにソックスを
はきなさい。
kutsu o haku maeni sokkusu o
hakinasai

to begin
はじめる hajimeru

She wants to begin the
painting.

かのじょはペンキをぬりはじ
めたい。
kanojo wa penki o nurihajimetai

behind
うしろに **ushiro-ni**

The boy is behind the tree.

そのしょうねんはそのきのうし
にいます。

sono shoonen wa sono ki no
ushiro-ni imasu

to believe
しんじる **shinjiru**

This is too good to believe.

これはあまりによすぎてしん
じられません。

kore wa amari ni yosugite
shinjiraremasen

bell
ベル **belu**

Don't ring that bell!

そのベルをならさないでください!
sono belu wo narasanaide kudasai

belt *See Clothing (page 24).*
ベルト **beluto**

berry
ベリー **berii**

Those berries look good.

これらのベリーはおいしそ
にみえる。

korera no berii wa oishisou
ni mieru

best
いちばんよい
ichiban yoi

The red box is the best.

そのあかいはこがいちばんよい。
sono akai hako ga ichiban yoi

better
よりよい **yori yoi**

The belt is better than
the pin.

そのベルトはそのピン
よりよい。
sono beluto wa sono pin
yori yoi

between
のであいだに
no aida ni

He is between two
trees.

かれはにほんのきの
あいだにいる。
kare wa nihon no ki no
aida ni iru

bicycle *See Transportation (page 108).*
じてんしゃ **jitensha**

big
おおきい **ookii**

He is very big.

かれはとてもおおきい。
kare wa totemo ookii

biking *See Games and Sports (page 44).*
サイクリング **saikuringu**

bird
とり **tori**

The bird is flying south for the winter.

そのとりはふゆにはみなみに
むかってとんでいます。

sono tori wa fuyu niwa minami ni mukatte tonde imasu

birthday
たんじょうび **tanjoobi**

Happy birthday!

たんじょうびおめでとう！

tanjoobi omedetoo!

black *See Numbers and Colors (page 68).*
くろ **kuro**

blank
なにもかかれていない

nanimo kakarete inai

The pages are blank.

そのページにはなにもかかれて
いません。

sono peeji niwa nani mo kakarete imasen

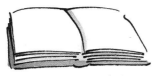

blanket
もうふ **moofu**

What is under that blanket?

もうふのしたにはなにが
ありますか？

moofu no shita niwa nani ga arimasuka?

blouse *See Clothing (page 24).*
ブラウス **bulausu**

to blow
ふく **fuku**

The wind is starting to blow.

かぜがふきはじめました。

kaze ga fukihajime mashita

blue *See Numbers and Colors (page 68).*
あお **ao**

boat *See Transportation (page 108).*
ボート **booto**

book
ほん **hon**

I am reading a book.

わたしはほんをよんで
います。

Watashi wa hon o yonde imasu

bookstore
ほんやさん **honya-san**

You can buy a book at a bookstore.

あなたはほんやさんでほんをかう
ことができます。

Anata wa honya-san de hon o kau kotoga dekimasu

boots *See Clothing (page 24).*
ブーツ **buutsu**

bottle
びん **bin**

The straw is in the bottle.

そのストローはそのビンのなか
にあります。

sono sutoroo wa sono bin no naka
ni arimasu

bowl
ボウル **boolu**

Some food is still in the bowl.

そのボウルのなかにはいくらかの
しょくもつがあります。

sono boolu no naka niwa ikuraka no
shokumotsu ga arimasu

bowling *See Games and Sports (page 44).*
ボウリング **boolingu**

box
はこ **hako**

Why is that fox in the box?

なぜそのきつねはそのはこのなかに
いるのですか?

naze sono kitsune wa sono hako no naka
ni iru nodesuka?

boy
しょうねん **shoonen**

The boys are twin brothers.

そのしょうねんたちはふたごです。

sono shoonen-tachi wa futago desu

branch
えだ **eda**

Oh, no! Get off that
branch!

ああ、だめ！そのえだから
たちさりなさい!

a-a dame! sono eda kara tachisarinasai!

brave
ゆうかんな **yuukan-na**

What a brave mouse!

なんてゆうかんなねずみだ!

nante yuukan na nezumi da!

bread
パン **pan**

He likes bread with jam
and butter.

かれはジャムとバターをぬった
パンがすきです。

kare wa jamu to bataa o nutta
pan ga sukidesu

to break
わる **waru**

It is easy to break an egg.

たまごをわるのはたやすい。

tamago o waru nowa tayasui

breakfast
あさごはん **asagohan**

Morning is the time
for breakfast.

あさはあさごはんのじかんです。

asa wa asagohan no jikan desu

bridge
はし hashi

The boat is under
the bridge.

そのボートはそのはしのしたに
います。
sono booto wa hashi no shita ni imasu

to bring
つれてゆく
turete yuku

She wants to bring
the lamb to school.

かのじょはこひつじを
がっこうにつれてゆきたい。
kanojo wa kohituji o gakko
ni turete yukitai

broom
ほうき hooki

A broom is for
sweeping.

ほうきははくための
ものです。
hooki wa hakutame no
mono desu

brother
にいさん niisan

He is my brother.

かれはぼくのにいさんです。
kare wa boku no niisan desu

brown *See Numbers and Colors (page 68).*
ちゃいろ chairo

brush
ブラシ burashi

I need my hairbrush.

わたしはじぶんのヘアブラシ
がひつようです。
watashi wa jibun no hea-burashi
ga hituyou desu

bubble
あわ awa

The bathtub is full of bubbles.

そのバスタブはあわでいっ
ぱいです。
sono basutabu wa awa de
ippai desu

bug
むし mushi

Do you know the
name of this bug?

あなたはこのむしのなま
えをしっていますか?
anata wa kono mushi no
namae wo shitte imasuka?

to build
つくる tukuru

I want to build a box.

わたしははこをつくりたい。
watashi wa hako o tukuritai

bus *See Transportation (page 108).*
バス **basu**

bush
しげみ **shigemi**

A bird is in the bush.

いっぴきのとりがそのしげみ
のなかにいます。
ippiki no tori ga sono shigemi
no naka ni imasu

busy
いそがしい **isogashii**

He is very busy.

かれはとてもいそがしい。
kare wa totemo isogashii

but
だが **daga**

The pencil is on the table,
but the book is on the chair.

そのえんぴつはそのテーブルの
うえにありますが、そのほんは
そのいすのうえにあります。
sono enpitsu wa sono teebulu no
ue ni arimasu ga sono hon wa
sono isu no ue ni arimasu

butter
バター **bataa**

Bread and butter
taste good.

パンとバターはおいしい。
pan to bataa wa oishii

butterfly *See Insects (page 52).*
ちょう **chyou**

button
ボタン **botan**

One button is missing.

ボタンがひとつなくなって
います。
botan ga hitotsu nakunatte imasu

to buy
かう **kau**

He wants to buy
a banana.

かれはいっぽんのバナナ
をかいたい。
kare wa ippon no banana
o kaitai

by
そばに **soba-ni**

She is standing
by the cheese.

かのじょはチーズの
そばにたっています。
kanojo wa cheezu no
soba-ni tatteimasu

cage
かご kago

The bird is on the cage.

そのとりはそのかごのうえ
にいます。
sono tori wa sono kago no ue
ni imasu

cake
ケーキ keeki

She likes to eat cake.

かのじょはケーキをたべる
のがすきです。
kanojo wa keeki o taberu
noga sukidesu

to call
でんわする denwa-suru

Remember to call me
again later.

あとでもういちどわすれずに
わたしにでんわしてください。
ato de moo ichido wasurezuni
watashi ni denwa sitekudasai

camel
らくだ rakuda

The camel is hot.

そのらくだはあつがっています。
sono rakuda wa atsugatte imasu

camera
カメラ kamera

Smile at the camera!

カメラにむかってほほえんで
ください!
kamera ni mukatte hohoende
kudasai!

can
かん kan

What is in that can?

あのかんのなかにはなに
がありますか?
ano kan no naka niwa nani
ga arimasuka?

candle
ろうそく rousoku

She is lighting the candle.

かのじょはろうそくにひ
をつけています。
kanojo wa rousoku ni hi
o tsukete imasu

candy
キャンデー kyandee

Candy is sweet.

キャンデーはあまい。
kyandee wa amai

cap *See Clothing (page 24).*
ぼうし booshi

car *See Transportation (page 108).*
じどうしゃ **jidooshya**

card
トランプ **toranpu**

Do you want to play cards?

トランプであそびたいですか？
toranpu de asobitai desuka?

to care
せわをする **sewa o-suru**

Her job is to care for pets.

かのじょのしごとはペット
たちのせわをすることです。
kanojo no shigoto wa petto tachi
no sewa o-suru kotodesu

carpenter
だいくさん **daiku-san**

A carpenter makes things
with wood.

だいくさんはきでものを
つくります。
daiku-san wa ki de mono o
tsukurimasu

carrot
にんじん **ninjin**

A carrot is orange.

にんじんはきいろい。
ninjin wa kiiroi

to carry
はこぶ **hakobu**

He carries a big bag.

かれはおもいふくろをひとつ
はこびます。
kare wa omoi fukuro o hitotsu
hakobimasu

castanets
カスタネット **kasutanetto**

Click the castanets to
the music!

おんがくにあわせてカスタネ
ットをならしてください！
ongaku ni awasete kasutanetto o
narashite kudasai!

castle
おしろ **oshiro**

The king lives in a castle.

そのおうさまはおしろの
なかにすんでいます。
sono oosama wa oshiro no
naka ni sunde imasu

cat
ねこ **neko**

The cat sees the
mouse.

そのねこはそのねずみ
をみています。
sono neko wa sono
nezumi o miteimasu

caterpillar *See Insects (page 52).*
けむし **kemushi**

to catch
つかまえる **tukamaeru**

He runs to catch the ball.

かれはそのボールをつかまえる
ためにはしります。
kare wa sono boolu o tsukamaeru
tameni hashirimasu

cave
ほらあな **horaana**

Who lives in the cave?

そのほらあなのなかにはだれが
すんでいますか?
sono horaana no naka niwa dare ga sunde imasuka?

to celebrate
おいわいをする
oiwai o-suru

They celebrate his birthday.

かれらはかれのたんじょうび
のおいわいをします。
karera wa kare no tanjoobi no
oiwai o simasu

chair
いす **isu**

He is sitting on a chair.

かれはいすのうえにすわっ
ています。
kare wa isu no ue ni suwatte imasu

chalk
チョーク **chyooku**

You can write with chalk.

あなたはチョークでかく
ことができます。
anata wa chyooku de kaku
kotoga dekimasu

to change
きがえる **kigaeru**

He wants to change his shirt.

かれはじぶんのシャツを
きがえたいとおもっています。
kare wa jibun no shatsu o
kigaetai to omotte imasu

to cheer
おうえんする **ooen-suru**

It is fun to cheer for our team.

じぶんたちのチームをおう
えんするのはたのしみです。
jibuntachi no chiimu o
ooen-suru nowa tanosimi desu

cheese
チーズ **chiizu**

The mouse likes to eat cheese.

そのねずみはチーズを
たべるのがすきです。
sono nezumi wa chiizu
o taberunoga sukidesu

Clothing
いふく
ifuku

vest
ベスト
besuto

hat
ぼうし
booshi

raincoat
レインコート
rein-kooto

cap
ぼうし
booshi

jacket
ジャケット
jaketto

earmuffs
イアマフ
iamafu

shirt
シャツ
shatsu

tie
ネクタイ
nekutai

pants
パンツ
pantsu

belt
ベルト
beluto

gloves
てぶくろ
tebukuro

socks
ソックス
sokkusu

sneakers
スニーカー
suniikaa

dress
ドレス
doresu

coat
コート
kooto

mittens
てぶくろ
tebukuro

boots
ブーツ
buutsu

scarf
スカーフ
sukaafu

blouse
ブラウス
bulausu

sweater
セーター
seetaa

skirt
スカート
sukaato

shoes
くつ
kutsu

shawl
ショール
shoolu

25

cherry
さくらんぼ **sakuranbo**

He wants a cherry.

かれはさくらんぼがほしい。
kare wa sakuranbo ga hoshii

chicken *See Animals (page 10).*
にわとり **niwatori**

child
こども **kodomo**

She is a happy child.

かのじょはゆかいなこどもです。
kanojo wa yukai na kodomo desu

chocolate
チョコレート **chokoleeto**

He likes chocolate.

かれはチョコレートがすきです。
kare wa chokoleeto ga sukidesu

circle
えん **en**

It is drawing a circle.

それはえんをえがいています。
sore wa en o egaite imasu

circus
サーカス **saakasu**

There are clowns at a circus.

サーカスにはピエロたちがいます。
saakasu niwa pierotachi ga imasu

city
まち **machi**

This cow does not live in the city.

このめうしはまちにすんでいません。
kono meushi wa machi ni sunde imasen

to clap
てをたたく **te o tataku**

He likes to clap when he is happy.

かれはしあわせなときにはてをたたくのがすきです。
kare wa shiawase na toki niwa te o tatakunoga sukidesu

class
クラス **kurasu**

There is an elephant in my class.

わたしのクラスにはぞうがいっぴきいます。
watashi no kurasu niwa zoo ga ippiki imasu

classroom
きょうしつ kyooshitu

A teacher works in a classroom.

せんせいはきょうしつではたらきます。
sensei wa kyooshitu de hatarakimasu

clock
めざましどけい
mezamashi-dokei

A clock tells time.

めざましどけいがときをつげます。
mezamashi-dokei ga toki o tsugemasu

clean
きれいな kireina

The car is very clean.

そのじどうしゃはとてもきれいです。
sono jidoosha wa totemo kireidesu

close
ちかくに chkaku-ni

The turtle is close to the rock.

そのかめはそのいわのちかくにいます。
sono kame wa sono iwa no chikaku ni imasu

to clean
そうじする sooji-suru

He is starting to clean his room.

かれはじぶんのへやをそうじしはじめています。
kare wa jibun no heya o sooji sihajimeteimasu

to close
しめる shimeru

He is going to close the window.

かれはまどをしめようとしています。
kare wa mado o shimeyou to shiteimasu

closet
おしいれ oshiire

See Rooms in a House (page 86).

to climb
のぼる noboru

The bear likes to climb the tree.

くまはきにのぼるのがすきです。
kuma wa ki ni noborunoga sukidesu

cloud
くも kumo

The sun is behind the cloud.

たいようはくもにかくれています。
taiyoo wa kumo ni kakurete imasu

clown
ピエロ piero

The clown is funny.

そのピエロはおもしろい。
sono piero wa omoshiroi

coat *See Clothing (page 24).*
コート kooto

cold
さむい samui

It is cold in here!

ここはさむい!
koko wa samui!

comb
くし kushi

Where is my comb?

ぼくのくしはどこ?
boku no kushi wa doko?

to comb
くしでとく kushi de toku

He likes to comb his hair.

かれはじぶんのかみをくしで
とくのがすきです。
kare wa jibun no kami wo kushi de
tokunoga sukidesu

to come
くる kuru

Come over here!

ここにきて!
koko ni kite!

computer
コンピューター konpyutaa

She is working at
her computer.

かのじょはじぶんのコンピュー
ターではたらいています。
kanojo wa jibun no konpyutaa de
hataraite imasu

to cook
りょうりをする
ryoori o-suru

It is fun to cook.

りょうりをするのはたのしい。
ryoori o-suru nowa tanoshii

cookie
クッキー kukkii

Mary wants a cookie.

メアリーはクッキーがほしい。
mearii wa kukkii ga hoshii

to count
かぞえる kazoeru

There are too many stars
to count.

かぞえきれないくらいおおくの
ほしがあります。
kazoekirenai kurai ooku no hoshi
ga arimasu

country
いなか inaka

The country is beautiful.

いなかはうつくしい。
inaka wa utsukushii

cow *See Animals (page 10).*
めうし meushi

crayon
えんぴつ enpitsu

She is drawing with her crayons.

かのじょはじぶんのえん
ぴつでえをかいています。
kanojo wa jibun no enpitsu
de e o kaiteimasu

cricket *See Games and Sports (page 44).*
クリケット kuriketto

cricket *See Insects (page 52).*
コオロギ koorogi

crowded
ひとがいっぱい
hito ga ippai

This elevator is crowded.

このエレベーターはひとが
いっぱいです。
kono elebeetaa wa hito ga ippai desu

to cry
なく naku

Try not to cry!

なかないようにしなさい!
nakanai yooni shinasai!

cup
コップ koppu

He is drinking water from the cup.

かれはそのコップでみ
ずをのんでいます。
kare wa sono koppu de
mizu o nonde imasu

to cut
きざむ kizamu

Use a knife to cut the carrots!

にんじんをきざむためにナイ
フをつかいなさい!
ninjin wo kizamu tameni naifu
o tukainasai!

cute
かわいい kawaii

She thinks her baby is cute.

かのじょはじぶんのあかちゃん
がかわいいとおもっています。
kanojo wa jibun no akachan ga
kawaii to omotte imasu

D

dad
パパ papa

My dad and I look alike.

ぼくのパパとぼくはにています。
boku no papa to boku wa
nite imasu

to dance
おどる odoru

The pig likes to dance
and play the drum.

そのぶたはおどってドラム
をたたくのがすきです。
sono buta wa odotte doramu
o tatakunoga sukidesu

danger
きけん kiken

He is in danger.

かれにはきけんがせまっ
ています。
kare niwa kiken ga sematte
imasu

dark
くらい kurai

It is dark at night.

よるはくらい。
yoru wa kurai

day
ひるま hiruma

The sun shines in the day.

たいようはひるまてります。
taiyoo wa hiruma terimasu

December
じゅうにがつ
juunigatsu

The month after
November is December.

じゅういちがつのつぎのつ
きはじゅうにがつです。
juuichigatsu no tugi no tuki
wa juunigatsu desu

to decide
きめる kimeru

It is hard to decide.

きめるのはむずかしい。
kimeru nowa muzukashii

decision
けってい kettei

That is a good decision.

それはよいけっていです。
sore wa yoi kettei desu

deck *See Rooms in a house (page 86)*
ベランダ beranda

decorations
かざりつけ kazaritsuke

The decorations look great!

そのかざりつけはすてきな
ようだ!
sono kazaritsuke wa suteki na yooda!

deer
しか shika

The deer is running
in the woods.

そのしかはそのもりのなか
をはしっています。
sono shika wa sono mori no naka
o hashitte imasu

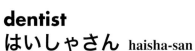

dentist
はいしゃさん haisha-san

The dentist has a big job.

そのはいしゃさんはおおしごとです。
sono haisha-san wa ohshigoto desu

department
うりば uriba

This is the hat
department.

ここがぼうしのうりばです。
koko ga booshi no uriba desu

desk
つくえ tukue

The desk is very messy.

そのつくえはとてもちらかって
います。
sono tukue wa totemo chirakatte imasu

different
ちがっている
chigatte-iru

The one in the middle
is different.

まんなかのものはちがっています。
mannaka no mono wa chigatte imasu

difficult
むずかしい muzukashii

This is difficult!

これはむずかしい!
kore wa muzukashii!

to dig
ほる horu

A dog uses its paws to dig.

いぬはほるためにじぶんの
あしをつかいます。
inu wa horutame ni jibun no
ashi o tsukaimasu

dining room *See Rooms in a House (page 86).*
ダイニングルーム dainingu-ruumu

dinner
ばんごはん bangohan

We have dinner at 6 o'clock.

わたしたちはろくじにば
んごはんをたべます。
watashitachi wa rokuji ni
bangohan o tabemasu

dinosaur
きょうりゅう
kyooryuu

The dinosaur is having fun.

そのきょうりゅうはあそんでいます。
sono kyooryuu wa asonde imasu

D

dirty
きたない kitanai

The pig is dirty.

そのぶたはきたない。
sono buta wa kitanai

dish
さら sara

Do not drop the dishes!

さらをおとさないでください!
sara wo otosanaide kudasai!

to do
するべき surubeki

He has a lot to do.

かれはするべきことがたくさん
あります。
kare wa surubeki koto ga takusan
arimasu

doctor
おいしゃさん oisha-san

The doctor checks
the baby.

そのおいしゃさんはそのあか
ちゃんをしんさつしています。
sono oisha-san wa sono akachan
o shinsatsu siteimasu

dog
いぬ inu

The dog has a funny hat.

そのいぬはおもしろいぼうしを
かぶっています。
sono inu wa omoshiroi booshi o
kabutte imasu

doll
にんぎょう ningyoo

The doll is in a box.

そのにんぎょうははこの
なかにあります。
sono ningyoo wa hako no
naka ni arimasu

dolphin
イルカ iruka

Dolphins live in the sea.

イルカはうみにすんでいます。
iruka wa umi ni sunde imasu

donkey
ロバ roba

The donkey is sleeping.

そのロバはねむっています。
sono roba wa nemutte imasu

door
ドア doa

What is behind the door?

そのドアのうしろになにが
ありますか?
sono doa no ushiro ni nani ga
arimasuka?

down
おりて orite

The elevator is
going down.

そのエレベーターはおりて
います。
sono elebeetaa wa orite imasu

dragon
りゅう **ryuu**

The dragon is cooking lunch.

そのりゅうはランチをりょうり
しています。
sono ryuu wa lanchi o ryoori
shiteimasu

to draw
えをかく **e o kaku**

He likes to draw.

かれはえをかくことがすきです。
kare wa e o kaku koto ga sukidesu

drawing
え **e**

Look at my drawing!

ぼくのえをみてください!
boku no e o mitekudasai!

dress *See Clothing (page 24).*
ドレス **doresu**

to drink
のむ **nomu**

She likes to drink milk.

かのじょはミルクをのむのが
すきです。
kanojo wa miluku o nomunoga
sukidesu

to drive
うんてんする
unten-suru

He is too small to drive.

かれはおさなすぎてうん
てんできない。
kare wa osanasugite unten dekinai

to drop
おとす **otosu**

He is going to drop the pie.

かれはパイをおとしそうだ。
kare wa pai o otoshisoo da

drum
ドラム **doramu**

He plays the drum.

かれはドラムをえんそうします。
kare wa doramu o ensoo shimasu

dry
かわいた **kawaita**

The shirt is dry.

そのシャツはかわいています。
sono shatsu wa kawaite imasu

duck *See Animals (page 10).*
アヒル **ahiru**

dust
ごみ **gomi**

There is dust under the bed.

そのベッドのしたにはごみが
ちらかっています。
sono beddo no shita niwa gomi
ga chirakatte imasu

E

each
それぞれの sorezore no

Each snowflake is different.

それぞれのスノーフレークは
ことなっています。
sorezore no sunoo-fureeku wa
kotonatte imasu

ear *See People (page 76).*
みみ mimi

early
はやく hayaku

The sun comes up early
in the day.

たいようはあさはやくのぼります。
taiyoo wa asa hayaku noborimasu

earmuffs *See Clothing (page 24).*
イヤマフ iyamafu

to earn
かせぐ kasegu

We work to earn money.

わたしたちはおかねをかせぐ
ためにはたらきます。
watashitachi wa okane o kasegu tameni hatarakimasu

east
ひがし higashi

The sun comes up in the east.

たいようはひがしにのぼります。
taiyoo wa higashi ni noborimasu

to eat
たべる taberu

This bird likes to eat worms.

このとりはむしたちをたべるのが
すきです。
kono tori wa mushitachi o taberunoga
sukidesu

egg
たまご tamago

The hen has an egg.

そのメンドリはたまごをうんでいます。
sono mendori wa tamago o unde imasu

eight *See Numbers and Colors (page 68).*
はち hachi

eighteen *See Numbers and Colors (page 68).*
じゅうはち juuhachi

eighty *See Numbers and Colors (page 68).*
はちじゅう hachjuu

elephant *See Animals (page 10).*
ぞう zoo

eleven *See Numbers and Colors (page 68).*
じゅういち juuichi

empty から kara

The bottle is empty.

そのびんはからです。
sono bin wa kara desu

to end
おわらせる owaraseru

It is time to end the game.

そのゲームをおわらせる
ときです。
sono geemu wo owaraseru
toki desu

everything
すべてのもの
subete no mono

Everything is purple.

すべてのものがむらさ
きいろです。
subete no mono ga
murasaki-iro desu

enough
じゅうぶんな juubun na

He has enough food!

かれはじゅうぶんなたべもの
をもっています。
kare wa juubun na tabemono
o motte imasu

everywhere
いたるところに
itarutokoro-ni

There are balls everywhere.

いたるところにボールが
あります。
itarutokoro-ni boolu ga
arimasu

every
どの dono

Every egg is broken.

どのたまごもひびわれしています。
dono tamago mo hibiware shiteimasu

excited
こうふんしている koofun shiteiru

He is excited.

かれはこうふんしています。
kare wa koofun shiteimasu

everyone
みんな minna

Everyone here has spots!

ここではみんなたまもようです！
koko dewa minna tama-moyoo desu!

eye *See People (page 76).*
め me

F

face *See People (page 76).*
かお kao

factory
こうじょう koojyoo

Cans are made in this factory.

かんはこのこうじょうで
つくられます。
kan wa kono koojyoo de tsukuraremasu

to fall
たおれる taoreru

He is about to fall.

かれはたおれかかっています。
kare wa taorekakatte imasu

fall
あき aki

It is fall.

あきです。
aki desu

family
かぞく kazoku

This is a big family.

これはだいかぞくです。
kore wa dai kazoku desu

fan
せんぷうき senpuuki

Please, turn off the fan!

どうか、せんぷうきをとめて
ください!
dooka, senpuki wo tomete kudasai!

far
とおくに tooku-ni

The moon is far away.

つきははるかとおくに
あります。
tuki wa haruka tooku-ni arimasu

faraway
はるかとおくに
haruka tooku-ni

She is going to a faraway place.

かのじょははるかとおくのばしょ
にゆこうとしています。
kanojo wa haruka tooku no basho ni yukoo to shiteimasu

fast
はやく hayaku

That train is going fast!

そのでんしゃははやくはしって
います!
sono densha wa hayaku hashitte imasu!

fat
ふとって futotte

The pig is fat.

そのぶたはふとっています。
sono buta wa futotte imasu

father
おとうさん otoosan

My father and I look alike.

ぼくのおとうさんとぼくはにています。
boku no otoosan to boku wa nite imasu

favorite
おきにいりの okiniiri no

This is my favorite toy.

これはわたしのおきにいりの
にんぎょうです。
kore wa watashi no okiniiri no
ningyoo desu

feather はね hane

The feather is
tickling her nose.

そのはねがかのじょのはなを
くすぐっています。
sono hane ga kanojo no hana o
kusugutte imasu

February
にがつ nigatsu

The month after January is
February.

いちがつのつぎのつきは
にがつです。
ichigatsu no tugi no tsuki wa
nigatsu desu

to feel
かんじる kanjiru

He likes to feel safe.

かれはあんぜんにかんじる
ことがすきです。
kare wa anzen ni kanjiru
koto ga sukidesu

fence
かきね kakine

A zebra is on my fence.

わたしのかきねのうえに
いっぴきのシマウマがいます。
watashi no kakine no ue ni
ippiki no shimauma ga imasu

fifteen *See Numbers and Colors (page 68).*
じゅうご juugo

fifty *See Numbers and Colors (page 68).*
ごじゅう gojuu

to find
みつける mitukeru

He is trying to find his kite.

かれはじぶんのたこをみつけよう
としています。
kare wa jibun no tako wo mitukeyoo
to shiteimasu

finger *See People (page 76).*
ゆび yubi

fire
かじ kaji

He can put out the fire.

かれはかじをけせます。
kare wa kaji o kesemasu

F

firefighter
しょうぼうし shoobooshi

The firefighter has boots and a hat.

そのしょうぼうしはブーツとぼう
しをきています。
sono shoobooshi wa buutsu to
booshi wo kiteimasu

firefly *See Insects (page 52).*
ホタル hotaru

firehouse
しょうぼうしょ shooboosho

Welcome to the firehouse!

しょうぼうしょへようこそ!
shooboosho e yookoso!

first
はじめ hajime

The yellow one is first
in line.

そのきいろのものがれつ
のはじめです。
sono kiiro no mono ga retsu
no hajime desu

fish *See Animals (page 10).*
さかな sakana

five *See Numbers and Colors (page 68).*
ご go

to fix
しゅうりする

shyuuri -suru

She wants to fix it.

かのじょはそれをしゅうり
したい。
kanojo wa sore wo shyuuri
shitai

flag はた hata

A flag is above her hat.

いちまいのはたがかのじょの
ぼうしのまうえにあります。
ichimai no hata ga kanojo no
booshi no maue ni arimasu

flat ぺっちゃんこ pettchanko

The tire is flat.

そのタイヤはぺっちゃ
んこです。
sono taiya wa pettchanko
desu

flea *See Insects (page 52).*
ノミ nomi

floor
ゆか yuka

There is a hole in the floor.

ゆかにひとつのあなが
あります。
yuka ni hitotsu no ana ga
arimasu

flower
はな hana

The flower is growing.

そのはなはそだっています。
sono hana wa sodatte imasu

flute
フルート fuluuto

Robert plays the flute.

ロバートはフルートをふきます。
robaato wa fuluuto o fukimasu

fly *See Insects (page 52).*
ハエ hae

to fly
とぶ tobu

The bee wants to fly.

そのミツバチはとびたいのです。
sono mitubachi wa tobitainodesu

fog
きり kiri

He is walking in the fog.

かれはきりのなかを
あるいています。
kare wa kiri no naka o
aruite imasu

food
たべもの tabemono

He eats a lot of food.

かれはたくさんのたべもの
をたべます。
kare wa takusan no tabemono
o tabemasu

foot *See People (page 76).*
あし ashi

for
のため no tame

This is for you.

これはあなたのためです。
kore wa anata no tame desu

to forget
わすれる wasureru

He does not want to
forget his lunch!

かれはじぶんのランチを
わすれようとはしません。
kare wa jibun no lanchi o
wasureyoo towa shimasen

fork
フォーク fooku

He eats with a fork.

かれはフォークをつか
ってたべます。
kare wa fooku o tsukatte
tabemasu

forty *See Numbers and Colors (page 68).*
しじゅう **shijuu**

four *See Numbers and Colors (page 68).*
し **shi**

fourteen *See Numbers and Colors (page 68).*
じゅうし **juushi**

fox *See Animals (page 10).*
きつね **kitsune**

friday
きんようび **kinyoobi**

On Friday, we go to the park.

きんようびに、わたしたちは
こうえんにゆきます。
kinyoobi ni watashitachi wa kooen ni yukimasu

friend
ともだち **tomodachi**

We are good friends.

ぼくたちはよいともだち
です。
boku tachi wa yoi tomodachi desu

frog *See Animals (page 10).*
かえる **kaeru**

front
まむかいに **mamukai-ni**

She sits in front of him.

かのじょはかれのまむかいに
すわります。
kanojo wa kare no mamukai ni suwarimasu

fruit
くだもの **kudamono**

Fruit is delicious.

くだものはおいしい。
kudamono wa oishii

full
いっぱい **ippai**

The cart is full of lizards.

そのカートはトカゲで
いっぱいです。
sono kaato wa tokage de ippai desu

fun
たのしみ **tanoshimi**

She is having fun.

かのじょはたのしんでいます。
kanojo wa tanoshinde imasu

funny
おもしろい **omoshiroi**

What a funny face!

なんておもしろいかおだ!
nante omoshiroi kao da!

game
ゲーム **geemu**

We are playing a game.

わたしたちはゲームを
しています。
watashitachi wa geemu o
shiteimasu

garage *See Rooms in a House (page 86).*
ガレージ **gareeji**

garden
にわ **niwa**

Roses are growing in
the garden.

バラがにわにはえています。
bara ga niwa ni haete imasu

gate
もん **mon**

The gate is open.

そのもんはあいています。
sono mon wa aite imasu

to get
えようと **eyou-to**

The mice are trying to get
the cheese.

ねずみたちはチーズをえようと
しています。
nezumitachi wa chiizu wo eyou-to
shiteimasu

giraffe *See Animals (page 10).*
キリン **kirin**

girl
しょうじょ **shoojo**

The girl is dancing.

そのしょうじょはおどっています。
sono shoojo wa odotte imasu

to give
あげる **ageru**

I want to give you a
present.

ぼくはきみにプレゼント
をあげたい。
boku wa kimi ni purezento
o agetai

glad
うれしい **ureshii**

She is glad to see you.

かのじょはあなたに
あえてうれしい。
kanojo wa anata ni
aete ureshii

glass
ガラス galasu

Windows are made of glass.

まどはガラスでできています。
mado wa galasu de dekite imasu

glasses
めがね megane

This owl wears glasses.

このフクロウはめがねを
かけています。
kono fukurou wa megane o
kakete imasu

gloves *See Clothing (page 24).*
てぶくろ teburkuro

to go いく iku

It is time to go to your
room.

あなたのへやにいくとき
です。
anata no heya ni iku toki
desu

goat *See Animals (page 10).*
やぎ yagi

golf *See Games and Sports (page 44).*
ゴルフ golufu

good
やさしい yasashii

What a good dog!

なんてやさしいいぬだ!
nante yasashii inu da!

good-bye
さようなら sayoonara

Good-bye!

さようなら!
sayoonara!

goose
ガチョウ gachou

A goose is riding a
bicycle.

いちわのガチョウがじてんしゃ
にのっています。
ichiwa no gachou ga jitensha
ni notte imasu

gorilla
ゴリラ gorila

The gorilla is eating a banana.

そのゴリラはバナナをいっぽん
たべています。
sono gorila wa banana o ippon
tabete imasu

to grab
つかむ tsukamu

She wants to grab the
bananas.

かのじょはそのバナナを
つかみたい。
kanojo wa sono banana wo
tsukamitai

grandfather
おじいさん ojiisan

I have fun with
my grandfather!

ぼくはおじいさんといっしょ
でうれしい。
boku wa ojiisan to issho
de ureshii!

grandma
おばあちゃん obaachan

Grandma is my dad's mother.

おばあちゃんはぼくのパパ
のおかあさんです。
obaachan wa boku no papa
no okaasan desu

grandmother
おばあさん obaasan

My grandmother likes
to bake.

わたしのおばあさんはやく
のがすきです。
watashi no obaasan wa yaku
noga sukidesu

grandpa
おじいちゃん ojiichan

Grandpa is my
mom's father.

おじいちゃんはわたしのママ
のおとうさんです。
ojiichan wa watashi no mama
no otoosan desu

grape
ぶどう budou

Get the grapes!

そのぶどうをつかみなさい！
sono budou wo tukaminasai!

grass
くさ kusa

Cows eat grass.

めうしはくさをたべます。
meushi wa kusa o tabemasu

grasshopper *See Insects (page 52).*
キリギリス kirigirisu

Games and Sports
ゲームとスポーツ
geemu to supootsu

baseball
やきゅう
yakyuu

basketball
バスケットボール
basuketto-boolu

golf
ゴルフ
golufu

ping-pong
ピンポン
pin-pon

running
ランニング
ranningu

bowling
ボーリング
boolingu

soccer
サッカー
sakkaa

ice skating
アイススケート
aisusukeeto

tennis
テニス
tenisu

skiing
スキー
sukii

biking
サイクリング
saikuringu

swimming
すいえい
suiei

gray *See Numbers and Colors (page 68).*
はいいろ **haiiro**

great
すてきな **sutekina**

It is a great party.

すてきなパーティです。
sutekina paatii desu

green *See Numbers and Colors (page 68).*
みどり **midori**

groceries
ざっか **zakka**

The groceries are falling out.

そのざっかはこぼれおちています。
sono zakka wa koboreochite imasu

ground
つち **tuchi**

They live in the ground.

かれらはつちのなかに
すんでいます。
karera wa tuchi no naka ni
sunde imasu

group
グループ **guruupu**

This is a group of artists.

これはげいじゅつかたち
のグループです。
kore wa geijutsuka-tachi
no guruupu desu

to grow
せいちょうする
seichoo-suru

He wants to grow.

かれはせいちょうしたい。
kare wa seichoo shitai

to guess
あてる **ateru**

It is fun to guess what is inside.

なかになにがあるかを
あてるのはたのしみです。
naka ni nani ga aruka o
aterunowa tanoshimi desu

guitar
ギター **gitaa**

My robot plays the guitar.

わたしのロボットがギター
をひいています。
watashi no robotto ga gitaa
o hiite imasu

hair *See People (page 76).*
かみのけ kamino ke

half はんぶん **hambun**

Half the cookie is gone.

そのクッキーのはんぶんはたいらげた。
sono kukkii no hambun wa tairageta

hall *See Rooms in a House (page 86).*
ホール hoolu

hammer
ハンマー **hanmaa**

Hit the nail with the hammer!

ハンマーでくぎをうち なさい!
hanmaa de kugi o uchi nasai!

hammock
ハンモック hanmokku

Dad is sleeping in the hammock.

パパはハンモックでねています。
papa wa hanmokku de nete imasu

hand *See People (page 76).*
て te

happy
たのしい tanoshii

This is a happy face.

これはたのしいかおです。
kore wa tanoshii kao desu

hard
かたい katai

The rock is hard.

そのいわはかたい。
sono iwa wa katai

harp ハープ haapu

She plays the harp very well.

かのじょはとてもじょうずに ハープをひきます。
kanojo wa totemo joozu ni haapu o hikimasu.

hat *See Clothing (page 24).*
ぼうし booshi

to have もつ motsu

She needs to have three hats.

かのじょはみっつの ぼうしをもつこと がひつようです。
kanojo wa mittsu no booshi wo motu koto ga hituyou desu

he かれ kare

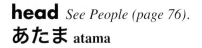

He is under the table.

かれはそのテーブルのしたに います。
kare wa sono teebulu no shita ni imasu

head *See People (page 76).*
あたま atama

to hear *See People (page 76).*
きく kiku

heart
ハート haato

The heart is red.

そのハートはあかい。
sono haato wa akai

helicopter *See Transportation (page 108).*
ヘリコプター helikoputaa

hello
こんにちは konnichiwa

Hello. How are you?

こんにちは。げんきですか?
konnichiwa. genki desuka?

help
たすけ tasuke

I need help!

たすけて!
tasukete!

her
かのじょの kanojo-no

This is her tail.

これはかのじょのしっぽです。
kore wa kanojo-no shippo desu

here
ここに kokoni

I live here.

わたしはここにすんでいます。
watashi wa koko ni sunde imasu

hi
やあ yaa

Hi!

やあ!
yaa!

to hide
かくれる kakureru

She is too big to hide under the box.

かのじょはおおきすぎてその
はこのしたにかくれられない。
kanojo wa ookisugite sono hako no
shita ni kakurerarenai

high
たかくに takaku-ni

The star is high in the sky.

そのほしはそらたかくにある。
sono hoshi wa sora takaku-ni aru

hill
おか oka

She is coming down the hill.

かのじょはおかを
くだっている。
kanojo wa oka o kudatte iru

hippopotamus *See Animals (page 10).*
ヒポポタマス **hipopotamasu**

to hit
うつ **utsu**

He tries to hit the ball.

かれはそのボールをうとうとしている。
kare wa sono boolu wo utoo to shiteiru

to hold
もつ **motsu**

He has to hold her hand now.

かれはいまかのじょのてを
もたなければなりません。
kare wa ima kanojo no te o
motanakereba narimasen

hole
あな **ana**

He is digging a hole.

かれはひとつのあなを
ほっています。
kare wa hitotsu no ana
o hotte imasu

hooray
ばんざい **banzai**

We are winning! Hooray!

ぼくたちはかっている!
ばんざい!
bokutachi wa katteiru! banzai!

to hop
とぶ **tobu**

They know how to hop.

かれらはとびかたをしっています。
karera wa tobikata o shitte imasu

horse *See Animals (page 10).*
うま **uma**

hospital
びょういん **byooin**

Doctors work at the hospital.

おいしゃさんたちはびょういんで
はたらきます。
oishasan-tachi wa byooin de hatarakimasu

hot
あつい **atsui**

Fire is hot.

ひはあつい。
hi wa atsui

hotel
ホテル **hotelu**

He is staying at
the hotel.

かれはそのホテルに
とまっています。
kare wa sono hotelu ni
tomatte imasu

hour
じかん jikan

In an hour, it is going
to be two o'clock.

いちじかんたてば、
にじになります。
ichijikan tateba, niji ni narimasu

house
いえ ie

The house has many windows.

そのいえにはたくさんのまど
があります。
sono ie niwa takusan no mado
ga arimasu

how
どうやって do yatte

How does he do that?

かれはどうやってそれをするの?
kare wa do yatte sore wo suruno?

hug
だく daku

Give me a hug!

だいてください!
daite kudasai!

huge
とてもおおきい
totemo ookii

That cat is huge!

そのねこはとてもおおきい!
sono neko wa totemo ookii!

hundred *See Numbers and Colors (page 68).*
ひゃく hyaku

(to be) hungry
おなかが（すく）
onaka ga (suku)

I think he is hungry.

わたしはかれがおなかが
すいているとおもいます。
watashi wa kare ga onaka ga suite iru to omoimasu

to hurry
いそぐ isogu

She has to hurry.

かのじょはいそがなければ
なりません。
kanojo wa isoganakereba
narimasen

to hurt
きずつける
kizu-tsukeru

It does not have to hurt.

それはきずつけては
なりません。
sore wa kizu tsukete wa
narimasen

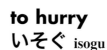

husband
おっと otto

He is her husband.

かれはかのじょのおっとです。
kare wa kanojo no otto desu

I
わたし watashi

"I am so cute!" she says.

「わたしってとてもかわいい!」
とかのじょはいいます。
"watashitte totemo kawaii!"
to kanojo wa iimasu

ice
こおり koori

We skate on ice.

わたしたちはこおりのうえで
アイススケートをします。
watashitachi wa koori no ue de
aisusukeeto o shimasu

ice cream
アイスクリーム aisukuriimu

Clara likes ice cream.

クララはアイスクリームがすきです。
kurara wa aisukuriimu ga sukidesu

idea
アイデア aidea

She has an idea.

かのじょはアイデアをもっています。
kanjo wa aidea o motte imasu

important
えらい erai

He looks very important.

かれはとてもえらくみえます。
kare wa totemo eraku miemasu

in
なかに naka-ni

What is in that box?

そのはこのなかには
なにがありますか?
sono hako no naka ni
wa nani ga arimasuka?

inside
なかに naka-ni

He is inside the house.

かれはいえのなかにいます。
kare wa ie no naka ni imasu

into
なかへ naka-e

Do not go into that cave!

そのほらあなのなかへ
はいっちゃだめ!
sono horaana no naka e
haittcha dame!

island
しま shima

The goat is on an island.

そのやぎはひとつのしまの
うえにいます。
sono yagi wa hitotsu no
shima no ue ni imasu

Insects
むしたち
mushi-tachi

wasp
カリバチ
karibachi

mantis
カマキリ
kamakiri

butterfly
ちょう
chyoo

flea
ノミ
nomi

fly
ハエ
hae

beetle
カブトムシ
kabutomushi

mosquito
か
ka

caterpillar
けむし
kemushi

grasshopper
キリギリス
kirigirisu

moth
が
ga

bee
はち
hachi

termite
シロアリ
shiroari

firefly
ホタル
hotalu

cricket
クリケット
kuriketto

ant
あり
ari

53

J

jacket *See Clothing (page 24).*
ジャケット **jaketto**

jaguar *See Animals (page 10).*
ヒョウ **hiyoo**

jam ジャム **jamu**

Do you think she likes bread and jam?

あなたはかのじょがパンとジャム
がすきだとおもいますか？
anata wa kanojo ga pan to jamu
ga sukidato omoimasuka?

January
いちがつ **ichigatsu**

January is the first month of the year.

いちがつはとしのはじめのつきです。
ichigatsu wa toshi no hajime no tsuki desu

jar ポット **potto**

Jam comes in a jar.

ジャムをいっぽんのポットにいれます。
jamu o ippon no potto ni iremasu

job しごと **shigoto**

It is a big job.

それはおおしごとだ。
sore wa ooshigoto da

juice
ジュース **jyuusu**

She is pouring a glass of orange juice.

かのじょはいっぱいの
オレンジジュースをそそぎます。
kanojo wa ippai no orenji juyuusu o sosogimasu

July
しちがつ **shitigatsu**

The month after June is July.

ろくがつのつぎのつきは
しちがつです。
rokugatsu no tugi no tuki wa
shitigatsu desu

to jump
とびはねる **tobihaneru**

She loves to jump.

かのじょはとびはねるのが
すきです。
kanojo wa tobihaneru noga
sukidesu

June
ろくがつ **rokugatsu**

The month after May is June.

ごがつのつぎのつきは
ろくがつです。
gogatsu no tugi no tuki wa
rokugatsu desu

junk
はいひん **haihin**

No one can use this junk.

だれもこのはいひんをつかえ
ません。
dare mo kono haihin o tsukaemasen

kangaroo *See Animals (page 10).*
カンガルー kangaruu

to keep
まもる mamoru

I want to keep him.

ぼくはかれをまもりたい。
boku wa kare wo mamoritai

key
かぎ kagi

Which key opens the lock?

どのかぎがそのロックを
あけますか?
dono kagi ga sono lokku
o akemasuka?

to kick
ける keru

He wants to kick
the ball.

かれはそのボール
をけりたい。
kare wa sono
boolu o keritai

kind
しんせつな shinsetsu na

She is kind to animals.

かのじょはどうぶつたち
にしんせつです。
kanojo wa doobutsu-tachi
ni shinsetsu desu

kind
しゅるい shyurui

What kind of animal is that?

それはどんなしゅるいの
どうぶつですか?
sore wa donna shyurui no
doobutsu desuka?

king
おうさま oosama

The king is having fun.

そのおうさまはたのしんで
います。
sono oosama wa tanoshinde imasu

kiss
キス kisu

Would you like to give
the monkey
a kiss?

あなたはそのさるにキス
したいですか?

anata wa sono saru ni kisu
shitaidesuka?

kitchen *See Rooms in a House (page 86).*
キッチン **kittchin**

kite
たこ **tako**

Kites can fly high.

たこはたかくあがること
ができます。
tako wa takaku agaru koto
ga dekimasu

kitten
こねこ **koneko**

A kitten is a baby cat.

こねこはあかちゃんねこ
です。
koneko wa akachan-neko
desu

knee *See People (page 76).*
ひざ **hiza**

knife
ナイフ **naifu**

A knife can cut.

ナイフはきることができます。
naifu wa kirukotoga dekimasu

to knock
ノックする **nokku-suru**

He starts to knock on
the door.

かれはそのドアをノック
しはじめる。
kare wa sono doa o nokku
shihajimeru

to know
しる **shiru**

He wants to know
what it says.

かれはなにがかかれてい
るのかをしりたい。
kare wa naniga kakarete
iru noka o shiritai

ladder
はしご **hashigo**

He climbs the ladder.

かれはそのはしごをのぼります。
kare wa sono hashigo o noborimasu

lake
みずうみ **mizuumi**

He is drinking the lake!

かれはそのみずうみをのんで
います。
kare wa sono mizuumi o nonde imasu

lamp
ランプ **lanpu**

He has a lamp on his head.

かれはじぶんのあたまのうえにランプ
をつけています。
kare wa jibun no atama no ue ni lanpu
o tsukete imasu

lap
ひざ **hiza**

He sits on his grandma's lap.

かれはかれのおばあちゃんのひざ
のうえにすわります。
kare wa kare no obaachan no hiza
no ue ni suwarimasu

last
いちばんうしろ
ichiban ushiro

The pink one is last in line.

そのピンクいろのものがれつの
いちばんうしろです。
sono pinku-iro no mono ga retsu no
ichiban ushiro desu

late
おそい **osoi**

It is late at night.

よるおそいです。
yoru osoi desu

to laugh
わらう **warau**

It is fun to laugh.

わらうのはたのしいです。
warau nowa tanoshii desu

laundry room
See Rooms in a House (page 86).
ランドリールーム **landorii-ruumu**

lazy
なまけて **namakete**

He is so lazy.

かれはとてもなまけて
います。
kare wa totemo namakete
imasu

leaf
はっぱ **happa**

The tree has one leaf.

そのきにははっぱがいちまい
あります。
sono ki niwa happa ga ichimai
arimasu

L

to leave
でかける dekakeru

She does not want to leave.

かのじょはでかけたくないです。
kanojo wa dekaketaku naidesu

left
ひだり hidari

This is your left hand.

これはあなたのひだりてです。
kore wa anata no hidari-te desu

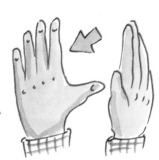

leg *See People (page 76).*
あし ashi

lemon
レモン lemon

She likes lemons.

かのじょはレモンがすきです。
kanojo wa lemon ga sukidesu

leopard
レオパード leopaado

A leopard is losing its spots.

いっぴきのレオパードはたまもようをなくしています。
ippiki no leopaado wa tama-moyoo o nakushite imasu

to let
させる saseru

Papa is not going to let him go.

パパはかれをゆかせようとはしません。
papa wa kare o yukaseyou towa shimasen

letter
てがみ tegami

This letter is going airmail.

このてがみはこうくうびんでとどけられます。
kono tegami wa kookuubin de todokeraremasu

library
としょかん toshokan

The library is full of books.

そのとしょかんはほんでいっぱいです。
sono toshokan wa hon de ippai desu

to lick
なめる nameru

You have to lick it.

あなたはそれをなめなければなりません。
anata wa sore o namenakereba narimasen

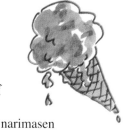

life
じんせい jinsei

Life is wonderful!

じんせいはすばらしい!
jinsei wa subarashii!

light
ひかり hikari

The sun gives us light.

たいようはわたしたちにひかり
をあたえます。
taiyoo wa watashitachi ni hikari
o ataemasu

lightning
いなずま inazuma

Look! There's lightning!

みて!いなずまだ!
mite! inazumada!

to like
すきです sukidesu

He likes the cake.

かれはそのケーキが
すきです。
kare wa sono keeki ga
sukidesu

like
のように no yooni

She looks like a rock.

かのじょはいわのように
みえます。
kanojo wa iwa no yooni
miemasu

line
せん sen

I can draw a line.

わたしはいっぽんのせんをかく
ことができます。
watashi wa ippon no sen o kaku
koto ga dekimasu

lion *See Animals (page 10).*
ライオン laion

to listen きく kiku

He does not want to
listen to loud music.

かれはさわがしいおんがく
をききたくはありません。
kare wa sawagashii ongaku
o kikitaku wa arimasen

little
ちいさい chiisai

The bug is little.

そのむしはちいさい。
sono mushi wa chiisai

to live すむ sumu

What a nice place to live!

すむにはなんてよいばしょだ!
sumu niwa nante yoi basho da!

living room
See Rooms in a House (page 86).
リビングルーム libingu-ruumu

llama *See Animals (page 10).*
ラマ lama

L

to lock
かぎをかける
kagi wo kakeru

Do not forget to lock the door.

ドアにかぎをかけるの
をわすれないでください。
doa ni kagi o kakeruno
o wasurenaide kudasai

long ながい nagai

That is a long snake.

それはながいへびです。
sore wa nagai hebi desu

to look ながめる nagameru

I use this to look at the stars.

わたしはほしたちをながめる
のにこれをつかいます。
watashi wa hoshitachi o nagameru
noni kore o tsukaimasu

to lose うしなう ushinau

He does not want to lose his hat.

かれはじぶんのぼうしを
うしないたくありません。
kare wa jibun no booshi o
ushinaitaku arimasen

lost
みちにまよって
michi ni mayotte

Oh, no! He is lost.

ああ、いけない! かれはみち
にまよっている。
aa ikenai! kare wa michi
ni mayottte iru

lots
たくさん takusan

There are lots of bubbles.

あわがたくさんあります。
awa ga takusan arimasu

loud
うるさい urusai

The music is loud!

そのおんがくはうるさい!
sono ongaku wa urusai!

to love すく suku

She loves the present.

かのじょはそのプレゼン
トがすきです。
kanojo wa sono purezento
ga sukidesu

love あい ai

Love is wonderful.

あいはすばらしい。
ai wa subarashii

low ひくい hikui

The bridge is low.

そのはしはひくい
sono hashi wa hikui

lunch ランチ lanchi

He has nuts for lunch.

かれはランチにきのみをた
べます。
kare wa lanchi ni kinomi o
tabemasu

mad
おこって okotte

The frogs are mad.

そのかえるたちはおこっています。
sono kaeru-tachi wa okotte imasu

mail
てがみ tegami

The mail is here.

さあ、てがみですよ。
saa tegami desuyo

mailbox
ゆうびんばこ
yuubin-bako

What is in that mailbox?

そのゆうびんばこのなかにはなにがありますか?
sono yuubin-bako no naka niwa nani ga arimasuka?

mail carrier
ゆうびんやさん
yuubinya-san

Our mail carrier brings us the mail.

わたしたちのゆうびんやさんがわたしたちにてがみをとどけます。
watashitachi no yuubinya-san ga watashitachi ni tegami wo todokemasu

to make
つくる tsukuru

A belt is easy to make.

ベルトはつくりやすい。
beluto wa tsukuriyasui

man
おとこのひと
otoko-no-hito

The man is waving with his hand.

そのおとこのひとがてをふっています。
sono otoko-no-hito ga te o futte imasu

mango
マンゴ mango

He will eat the whole mango.

かれはそのマンゴをぜんぶたべるでしょう。
kare wa sono mango o zenbu taberudeshoo

mantis *See Insects (page 52).*
カマキリ kamakiri

many
たくさんの
takusan no

There are many dots!

たくさんのてんがあります!
takusan no ten ga arimasu

map
ちず chizu

The map shows where to go.

そのちずはゆくべきばしょをしめしています。
sono chizu wa yukubeki basho o shimeshite imasu

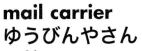

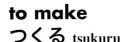

maraca
マラカス **marakasu**

Shake those maracas!

それらのマラカスをふってください!
sorerano marakasu o futte kudasai!

March
さんがつ **sangatsu**

The month after February is March.

にがつのつぎのつきはさんがつです。
nigatsu no tugi no tuki wa sangatsu desu

math
すうがく **suugaku**

He is not very good at math.

かれはすうがくがあまりとくい
ではありません。
kare wa suugaku ga amari tokui dewa arimasen

May
ごがつ **gogatsu**

The month after April is May.

しがつのつぎのつきはごがつです。
shigatsu no tugi no tuki wa gogatsu desu

maybe たぶん **tabun**

Maybe it is a ball.

たぶんそれはひとつのボールです。
tabun sore wa hitotsu no boolu desu

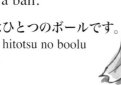

mayor
ちょうちょうさん
choochoo-san

The mayor leads the town.

そのちょうちょうさんがまちを
リードします。
sono choochoo-san ga machi o liido shimasu

me ぼくを **boku o**

Look at me!

ぼくをみて!
boku o mite!

to mean
いみする **imisuru**

That has to mean "hello."

それは「こんにちは」をいみ
するにちがいありません。
sore wa "konnichiwa" o imisuru ni chigai arimasen

meat にく **niku**

I am eating meat, salad, and potatoes for dinner.

わたしはディナーににく、
サラダとポテトをたべています。
watashi wa dinaa ni niku, salada to poteto o tabeteimasu

medicine
くすり **kusuri**

Take your medicine!

あなたのくすりをのみなさい!
anatano kusuri o nominasai!

to meet
あう au

I am happy to meet you.

あなたにあえてうれしいです。
anata ni aete ureshii desu

meow
ニャー nyaa

Cats say, "MEOW!"

ねこは「ニャー」となきます。
neko wa "nyaa" to nakimasu

mess
ちらかし chirakashi

What a mess!

なんというちらかし!
nanto iu chirakashi!

messy
だらしない darashinai

The bear is a little messy.

そのくまはちょっとだらしない。
sono kuma wa chotto darashinai

milk
ミルク miluku

He likes milk.

かれはミルクがすきです。
kare wea miluku ga sukidesu

minute
ふん fun

It is one minute before noon.

しょうごいっぷんまえです。
shoogo ippun mae desu

mirror
かがみ kagami

He loves to look in the mirror.

かれはかがみをながめるのが
すきです。
kare wa kagami o nagamerunoga
sukidesu

to miss
のりおくれる
noriokureru

He does not want to miss the airplane.

かれはそのひこうきに
のりおくれたくありません。
kare wa sono hikooki ni
noriokuretaku arimasen

mittens *See Clothing (page 24).*
てぶくろ tebukuro

to mix
かきまぜる kakimazeru

Use the spoon to mix it.

それをかきまぜるのにその
スプーンをつかいなさい。
sore o kakimazerunoni sono
supuun wo tukainasai

mom
ママ mama

She is the baby's mom.

かのじょはそのあかちゃん
のママです。

kanojo wa sono akachan
no mama desu

Monday
げつようび
getsuyoobi

Every Monday we take
a bath.

まいしゅうげつようびに
わたしたちはおふろに
はいります。

maishyuu getsuyoobi ni
watashitachi wa ofuro ni
hairimasu

money
おかね okane

Look at all the money!

そのおかねのぜんぶをみなさい!
sono okane no zenbu o minasai!

monkey *See Animals (page 10).*
さる saru

month
つき tsuki

January and February
are the first two months
of the year.

いちがつとにがつはとしの
さいしょのにかげつです。

ichigatsu to nigatsu wa toshi no
saisyo no nikagetsu desu

moon つき tsuki

The moon is up
in the sky.

つきがそらたかくでています。
tsuki ga soratakaku deteimasu

more
もっとたくさんの
motto takusan no

She needs to buy more juice.

かのじょはもっとたくさんの
ジュースをかうことが
ひつようです。

kanojo wa motto takusan no
juusu wo kau koto ga
hitsuyoo desu

morning あさ asa

The sun comes up
in the morning.

たいようはあさのぼります。
taiyoo wa asa noborimasu

mosquito *See Insects (page 52).*
か ka

most
ほとんどの hotondo-no

Most of the milk is gone.

ほとんどのミルクはからっぽです。
hotondo-no miluku wa karappo desu

moth *See Insects (page 52).*
が ga

mother
おかあさん okaasan

She is the baby's mother.

かのじょはそのあかちゃん
のおかあさんです。
kanojo wa sono akachan no okaasan desu

motorcycle *See Transportation (page 108).*
たんしゃ tansha

mountain やま yama

He is climbing up the mountain.

かれはそのやまにのぼっています。
kare wa sono yama ni nobotte imasu

mouse ねずみ nezumi

The mouse is skating.

そのねずみはスケートをしています。
sono nezumi wa sukeeto o shite imasu

mouth *See People (page 76).*
くち kuchi

to move
ひっこす hikkosu

They have to move.

かれらはひっこさなければなりません。
karera wa hikkosanakereba narimasen

movie えいが eiga

They are watching a movie.

かれらはえいがをみています。
karera wa eiga o miteimasu

Mr. さん san

Say hello to Mr. Green.

グリーンさんにあいさつしなさい。
Guriin-san ni aisatsu shinasai

Mrs. さん san

Mrs. Feront is getting on the bus.

フェロントさんはそのバス
にのろうとしています。
Feronto-san wa sono basu ni
norooto shiteimasu

much
たくさんの takusan no

There is not much food in the refrigerator.

れいぞうこにはたくさんの
しょくもつはありません。
reizooko niwa takusan no
syokumotsu wa arimasen

music
おんがく ongaku

They can play music.

かれらはおんがくをえんそう
できます。
karera wa ongaku o ensoo dekimasu

my
わたしの watashi no

This is my nose.

これはわたしのはなです。
kore wa watashi no hana desu

N

nail くぎ kugi

Try to hit the nail!

そのくぎをうってみて
ください。
sono kugi o utte mite kudasai

name なまえ namae

His name begins with "R."

かれのなまえは「R」ではじまります。
kare no namae wa"R"de hajimarimasu

neck *See People (page 76).*
くび kubi

necklace
ネックレス nekkulesu

She loves her necklace.

かのじょはじぶんのネックレス
がすきです。
kanojo wa jibun no nekkulesu
ga sukidesu

to need
ひつようとする
hitsuyouto-suru

He is going to need a snack later.

かれはあとでスナックがひつよう
なつもりです。
kare wa atode sunakku ga hitsuyou
na tsumori desu

neighbor
となりのひと
tonari no hito

They are neighbors.

かれらはとなりのひとびとです。
karera wa tonari no hitobito desu

nest す su

The birds are near their nest.

そのとりたちはじぶんたちの
すのちかくにいます。
sono tori-tachi wa jibuntachi no
su no chikaku ni imasu

never
けっして kesshite

She is never going to fly.

かのじょはけっしてとぼうとは
しません。
kanojo wa kesshite toboo towa shimasen

new
あたらしい atarashii

He has a new umbrella.

かれはあたらしいかさをもって
います。
kare wa atarashii kasa o motte imasu

newspaper
しんぶん shinbun

Who is cutting my newspaper?

だれがわたしのしんぶんを
きったのですか?
dare ga watashi no shinbun o
kittanodesuka?

next
そばに soba-ni

She is next to the rock.

かのじょはそのいわの
そばにいます。
kanojo wa sono iwa no
soba-ni imasu

next
つぎ tsugi

The horse is next.

そのうまがつぎです。
sono uma ga tsugi desu

nice
すてきな sutekina

What a nice clown!

なんてすてきなピエロだ!
nante sutekina piero da!

night
よる yoru

It is dark at night.

よるにはくらい。
yoru niwa kurai

nine *See Numbers and Colors (page 68).*
きゅう kyuu

nineteen *See Numbers and Colors (page 68).*
じゅうく jyuuku

ninety *See Numbers and Colors (page 68).*
きゅうじゅう kyuujyuu

no
だめ dame

No, you may not go.

だめ、あなたはゆけません。
dame, anata wa yukemasen

noise
さわがしいおと
sawagashii oto

He is making a terrible noise.

かれはとてもさわがしいおと
をたてています。
kare wa totemo sawagashii oto
wo tatete imasu

noisy
さわがしい sawagashii

They are very noisy.

かれらはとてもさわがしい。
karera wa totemo sawagashii

noon
しょうご shyoogo

It is noon.

しょうごです。
shyoogo desu

Numbers and Colors
かずといろ
kazu to iro

0 zero
ぜろ
zero

1 one
いち
ichi

2 two
に
ni

3 three
さん
san

4 four
し
shi

5 five
ご
go

6 six
ろく
roku

7 seven
しち
shichi

8 eight
はち
hachi

9 nine
きゅう
kyuu

10 ten
じゅう
jyuu

11 eleven
じゅういち
jyuuichi

12 twelve
じゅうに
jyuuni

 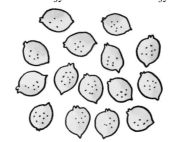 

13 thirteen
じゅうさん
jyuusan

14 fourteen
じゅうし
jyuushi

15 fifteen
じゅうご
jyuugo

16 sixteen
じゅうろく
jyuuroku

  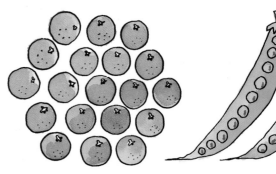

17 seventeen
じゅうしち
jyuushichi

18 eighteen
じゅうはち
jyuuhachi

19 nineteen
じゅうく
jyuuku

20 twenty
にじゅう
nijyuu

 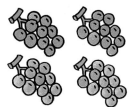  

30 thirty
さんじゅう
sanjyuu

40 forty
しじゅう
shijyuu

50 fifty
ごじゅう
gojyuu

60 sixty
ろくじゅう
rokujyuu

70 seventy
しちじゅう
shichijyuu

80 eighty
はちじゅう
hachijyuu

90 ninety
きゅうじゅう
kyuujyuu

100 one hundred
ひゃく
hyaku

1000 one thousand
せん
sen

Colors
いろ iro

black
くろ
kuro

blue
あお
ao

brown
ちゃいろ
chairo

gray
はいいろ
hai-iro

green
みどり
midori

orange
オレンジいろ
orenji-iro

pink
ピンクいろ
pinku-iro

purple
むらさき
murasaki

red
あか
aka

tan
ひやけのいろ
hiyake-no-iro

white
しろ
shiro

yellow
きいろ
kiiro

69

N

north
きた kita

It is cold in the north.

きたではさむい。
kita dewa samui

nose *See People (page 76).*
はな hana

not
ない nai

The bird is not red.

そのとりはあかくはないです。
sono tori wa akaku wa naidesu

note
メモ memo

He is writing a note.

かれはメモをかいています。
kare wa memo o kaiteimasu

nothing
なにも nanimo

There is nothing in the bottle.

そのびんのなかにはなにもありません。
sono bin no naka niwa nanimo arimasen

November
じゅういちがつ
jyuuichigatsu

The month after October is November.

じゅうがつのつぎのつきは
じゅういちがつです。
jyuugatsu no tugi no tuki wa jyuuichigatsu desu

now いま ima

The mouse needs to run now.

そのねずみはいまはしる
ひつようがあります。
sono nezumi wa ima hashiru hituyoo ga arimasu

number
かず kazu

There are five numbers.

いつつのかずがあります。
itsutsu no kazu ga arimasu

nurse
かんごし kangoshi

She wants to be a nurse.

かのじょはかんごしになりたいです。
kanojo wa kangoshi ni naritai desu

nut
きのみ kinomi

I think he likes nuts.

わたしはかれがきのみがすきだ
とおもいます。
watashi wa kare ga kinomi ga sukida to omoimasu

ocean
おおきなうみ ookina umi

This turtle swims in
the ocean.

このかめはそのおおきなうみ
でおよぎます。
kono kame wa sono ookina umi
de oyogimasu

o'clock
じ ji

It is one o'clock.

いちじです。
ichiji desu

October
じゅうがつ jyuugatsu

The month after September
is October.

くがつのつぎのつきは
じゅうがつです。
kugatsu no tsugi no tsuki wa
jyuugatsu desu

of の no

The color of the airplane
is yellow.

そのひこうきのいろはきいろです。
sono hikooki no iro wa kiiro desu

office *See Rooms in a House (page 86).*
オフィス ofuisu

oh
ああ aa

Oh! What a surprise!

ああ!なんてびっくり!
aa! nante bikkuri!

old
としおいた toshioita

The alligator is very old.

そのワニはとてもとしおいて
います。
sono wani wa totemo toshioite
imasu

on
うえに ue-ni

The coat is on the chair.

そのコートはそのいすの
うえにあります。
sono kooto wa sono isu no
ue-ni arimasu

once
いっかい ikkai

Birthdays come once a year.

たんじょうびはねんにいっかい
きます。
tanjyoobi wa nen ni ikkai
kimasu

one *See Numbers and Colors (page 68).*
いち ichi

onion
タマネギ tamanegi

He is chopping an onion.

かれはいっこのタマネギを
きざんでいます。
kare wa ikko no tamanegi o
kizandeimasu

only
ただひとつ
tadahitotsu

This is the only
food left.

これがただひとつのこって
いるたべものです。
kore ga tadahitotsu nokotte
iru tabemono desu

open
ひらいて hiraite

The window is open.

そのまどはひらいています。
sono mado wa hiraite imasu

or
か ka

Do you want the red
one or the blue one?

きみはあかいのがほしいのか
あおいのがほしいの?
kimi wa akai noga hoshii noka aoi noga hoshii no?

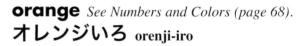

orange *See Numbers and Colors (page 68).*
オレンジいろ orenji-iro

orange
オレンジ orenji

He is squeezing oranges.

かれはオレンジをしぼっています。
kare wa orenji o shibotte imasu

ostrich
ダチョウ dachyoo

An ostrich can run fast.

ダチョウははやくはしれます。
dachyoo wa hayaku hashiremasu

other
むこう **mukoo**

What is on the other side?

むこうがわにはなにが
ありますか?
mukoogawa niwa nani ga
arimasuka?

ouch
いた **ita**

Ouch! That hurts!

いた! けがをする!
ita! kega o suru!

out(side)
そとへ **soto-e**

He goes out.

かれはでかけます。
kare wa dekakemasu

outdoors
アウトドアスポーツ
autodoa-supootsu

We like to play outdoors.

わたしたちはアウトドア-スポーツ
をするのがすきです。
watashitachi wa autodoa-supootsu
o suru noga sukidesu

oven
オーブン **oobun**

We bake cookies in
an oven.

わたしたちはオーブンでクッキー
をやきます。
watashitachi wa oobun de kukkii
o yakimasu

over
うえに **ue-ni**

She is holding the umbrella
over her head.

かのじょはじぶんのあたまの
うえにかさをもっています。
kanojo wa jibun no atama no
ue ni kasa o motteimasu

owl
フクロウ **fukurou**

The owl does not
sleep at night.

そのフクロウはよる
ねむりません。
sono fukurou wa yoru
nemurimasen

to own
てにいれる **te ni ireru**

It is wonderful to own a book.

いっさつのほんをてにいれるこ
とはすばらしい。
issatsu no hon o te ni ireru koto
wa subarashii

P

page ページ peeji

He is turning the page.

かれはそのページをめくっています。
kare wa sono peeji o mekutte imasu

paint ペンキ penki

The baby is playing with paint.

そのあかちゃんはペンキで
あそんでいます。
sono akachan wa penki de
asonde imasu

painter
えかきさん ekaki-san

He is a painter.

かれはえかきさんです。
kare wa ekaki-san desu

pajamas
パジャマ pajama

She is wearing pajamas to sleep.

かのじょはねるためにパジャマ
をきています。
kanojo wa neru tameni pajama
o kiteimasu

pan
フライパン furaipan

We cook with a pan.

わたしたちはフライパンで
りょうりをします。
watashitachi wa furaipan de
ryoori o shimasu

panda
パンダ panda

This panda is hungry.

このパンダはおなかが
すいています。
kono panda wa onakaga
suiteimasu

pants *See Clothing (page 24).*
パンツ pantsu

paper かみ kami

Write on the paper!

そのかみのうえにかきなさい!
sono kamino ue ni kakinasai!

parent おや oya

These parents have many babies.

これらのおやたちにはたくさん
のあかちゃんがいます。
korera no oyatachi niwa takusan
no akachan ga imasu

park
こうえん kooen

We like to go to the park.

わたしたちはそのこうえんに
ゆくのがすきです。
watashitachi wa sono kooen ni
yukunoga sukidesu

parrot
オウム oomu

This parrot can say, "Cracker!"

このオウムは「クラッカー!」
といえます。
kono oomu wa "kurakkaa!" to iemasu

part いちぶ ichibu

A wheel is part of the car.

しゃりんはじどうしゃのいちぶ
です。
shyarin wa jidoosha no ichibu desu

party パーティー paatii

The ants are having a party.

そのアリたちはパーティをしています。
sono aritachi wa paatii wo shiteimasu

to pat
なでる naderu

The baby tries to pat the dog.

そのあかちゃんはそのいぬをなで
ようとします。
sono akachan wa sono inu o nadeyoo
to shiteimasu

paw て te

He wants to shake paws.

かれはあくしゅしたいです。
kare wa akushyu shitai desu

pea
エンドウマメ
endoomame

He does not like to
eat peas.

かれはエンドウマメをたべ
るのはすきではありません。
kare wa endoomame o taberu
noga sukidewa arimasen

peach
モモ momo

Peaches grow on trees.

モモはきのうえでそだちます。
momo wa ki no ue de
sodachimasu

pen
まんねんひつ
mannenhitsu

The pen is leaking.

そのまんねんひつはもれています。
sono mannnenhitsu wa morete imasu

pencil
えんぴつ enpitsu

A pencil is for drawing.

えんぴつはかくための
ものです。
enpitsu wa kaku tame no
mono desu

ひとびと ・ あなたのからだ

hitobito • anata no karada

face
かお
kao

head
あたま
atama

stomach
い
i

knee
ひざ
hiza

foot
あし
ashi

leg
あし
ashi

eye
め
me

hair
け
ke

thumb
おやゆび
oya-yubi

neck
くび
kubi

arm
うで
ude

finger
ゆび
yubi

hand
て
te

76

ear
みみ
mimi

tooth
は
ha

nose
はな
hana

to see
みる
miru

to touch
さわる
sawaru

mouth
くち
kuchi

toe
つまさき
tsumasaki

to hear
きく
kiku

to smell
かぐ
kagu

to taste
あじわう
ajiwau

penguin
ペンギン pengin

There is a penguin in your sink.

あなたのながしだいのなかに
いっぴきのペンギンがいます。

anata no nagashidai no naka ni
ippiki no pengin ga imasu

people
ひとびと hitobito

These people are going up.

これらのひとびとはうえに
あがろうとしています。

korera no hitobito wa ue ni
agaroo to shiteimasu

pepper
コショウ koshyoo

She is using too much pepper.

かのじょはコショウをおおく
ふりかけすぎます。

kanojo wa koshyoo o ooku
furikakesugimasu

peppers カラシ karashi

Peppers are good to eat.

カラシはおいしくないです。
karashi wa oishikunai desu

perfume こうすい koosui

She is wearing perfume.

かのじょはこうすいをふりかけて
います。
kanojo wa koosui o furikakete imasu

pet ペット petto

This pig is a pet.

このぶたはいっぴきの
ペットです。
kono buta wa ippiki no
petto desu

photograph
しゃしん shashin

Look at the photograph!

そのしゃしんをみて!
sono shashin o mite!

piano ピアノ piano

He plays the piano very well.

かれはとてもじょうずに
ピアノをひきます。
kare wa totemo joozu ni
piano o hikimasu

to pick
つみとる tsumitoru

This dog likes to pick berries.

このいぬはベリーをつみとる
のがすきです。
kono inu wa berii wo tsumitoru
noga sukidesu

picnic
ピクニック pikunikku

They are having a picnic.

かれらはピクニック
をしています。
karera wa pikunikku
o shiteimasu

picture え e

This is a picture of a rabbit.

これはいっぴきのウサギのえです。
korewa ippiki no usagi no e desu

pie パイ pai

Who is eating the pie?

だれがそのパイをたべて
いるのですか?
dare ga sono pai o tabete
irunodesuka?

pig *See Animals (page 10).*
ぶた buta

pillow
まくら makura

A pillow is for sleeping.

まくらはねるためのものです。
makura wa nerutameno mono desu

ping-pong *See Games and Sports (page 44).*
ピンポン pinpon

pink *See Numbers and Colors (page 68).*
ピンクいろ pinku-iro

pizza
ピザ piza

We like to eat pizza.

わたしたちはピザを
たべるのがすきです。
watashitachi wa piza o taberunoga sukidesu

to place
かける kakeru

It is good to place glasses
on the nose.

はなのうえにめがねを
かければよいです。
hana no ue ni megane
o kakereba yoi desu

to plan
けいかくする keikaku-suru

It helps to plan ahead.

それはさきゆきをけいかくする
のにやくだちます。
sore wa sakiyuki o keikaku suru
noni yakudachimasu

to plant うえる ueru

He likes to plant nuts.

かれはきのみをうえる
のがすきです。
kare wa kinomi o ueru
noga sukidesu

to play あそぶ asobu

Do you want to play
with us?

あなたはわたしたちと
いっしょにあそびたい
ですか?
anata wa watashitachi to
issho ni asobitai desuka?

playground
うんどうじょう
undoojoo

Meet me at the playground!

そのうんどうじょうでわたしに
あってください!

sono undoojoo de watashi ni
atte kudasai!

playroom *See Rooms in a House (page 86).*
ゆうぎしつ **yuugishitsu**

please
どうか **dooka**

Please, feed me!

どうか、わたしにたべもの
をください!

dooka, watashi ni tabemono
wo kudasai!

pocket
ポケット **poketto**

What is in his pocket?

かれのポケットのなかにはなに
がありますか?

kare no poketto no naka niwa nani
ga arimasuka?

point
さき **saki**

It has a sharp point.

それはとがったさきを
もっています。

sore wa togatta saki o motteimasu

to point
ゆびさす **yubisasu**

It is not polite to point.

ゆびさすのはしつれいです。

yubisasu nowa shitsurei desu

police officer
おまわりさん **omawari-san**

The police officer helps us cross
the street.

そのおまわりさんがとおりを
よこぎるのにわたしたちを
てつだってくれます。

sono omawari-san ga toori o
yokogiru noni watashitachi o
tetsudatte kuremasu

police station
けいさつしょ **keisatsusho**

You can get help at the
police station.

あなたはけいさつしょで
たすけをえられます。

anata wa keisatsusho de
tasuke o eraremasu

polite
れいぎただしい **reigi-tadashii**

He is so polite!

かれはとてもれいぎ
ただしい!

kare wa totemo reigi-tadashii!

pond いけ **ike**

She fell into the pond.

かのじょはそのいけにおちた。

kanojo wa sono ike ni ochita

poor
びんぼうな **binboona**

This poor monkey does not have much money.

このびんぼうなさるはあまりおかね
をもっていません。
kono binboo na saru wa amari okane
o motte imasen

porch *See Rooms in a House (page 86).*
げんかん **genkan**

post office
ゆうびんきょく
yuubinkyoku

Letters go to the post office.

てがみはゆうびんきょくにゆ
きます。
tegami wa yuubinkyoku
ni yukimasu

pot
ポット **potto**

It is time to stir the pot.

そのポットをかきまぜるときです。
sono potto o kakimazeru toki desu

potato
ポテト **poteto**

These potatoes have eyes.

これらのポテトたちには
めがあります。
korera no poteto-tachi niwa
me ga arimasu

to pound
カンカンたたく
kankan tataku

Use a hammer to pound a nail.

くぎをカンカンたたくには
ハンマーをつかいなさい。
kugi o kankan tataku niwa hanmaa
o tukainasai

present
プレゼント **purezento**

Is the present for me?

そのプレゼントはわたし
のためですか?
sono purezento wa watashi
no tame desuka?

pretty
うつくしい **utsukushii**

It is not a pretty face.

それはうつくしいかおでは
ありません。
sore wa utsukushii kao dewa arimasen

prince
おうじさま **oojisama**

The prince is with his father.

そのおうじさまはかれのお
とうさんといっしょにいます。
sono oojisama ha kare no
otoosan to issho ni imasu

princess
おうじょさま **oojyosama**

This princess has big feet.

このおうじょさまはおおきな
あしをもっています。
kono oojyosama wa ookina
ashi o motteimasu

prize
しょう shyoo

Look who wins the prize.

だれがそのしょうをとるのか
ごらんなさい。
dare ga sono shyoo wo torunoka
gorannasai

proud
とくいで tokui de

She is proud of her
new hat.

かのじょはかのじょのぼうしで
とくいになっています。
kanojo wa kanojo no booshi de
tokui ni natteimasu

to pull
ひく hiku

We're trying to pull him up.

わたしたちはかれをひきあげよう
としています。
watashitachi wa kare o hikiageyoo
to shiteimasu

puppy
こいぬ koinu

The puppy is wet.

そのこいぬはぬれています。
sono koinu wa nurete imasu

purple *See Numbers and Colors (page 68).*
むらさき murasaki

purse
ハンドバック
handobakku

The purse is full.

そのハンドバックは
いっぱいです。
sono handobakku wa ippai desu

to push
おす osu

He needs to push hard.

かれはもっとつよくおすひつよう
があります。
kare wa motto tuyoku osu hitsuyoo
ga arimasu

to put
いれる ireru

Don't put your foot in
your mouth!

あなたのあしをあなたのくち
のなかにいれないでください!
anata no ashi o anata no kuchi
no naka ni irenaide kudasai!

puzzle
パズル pazuru

Can you put the puzzle
together?

あなたはそのパズルを
あつめられますか?
anata wa sono pazuru o
atsumeraremasuka?

quack
ガーガー gaa gaa

"Quack, quack!" sing the ducks.

「ガーガー」とそのアヒルたちはうたっています。

"gaa, gaa!" to sono ahirutachi wa utatte imasu

to quarrel
けんかする kenka suru

We do not like to quarrel.

わたしたちはけんかをしたくありません。

watashitachi wa kenka o shitaku arimasen

quarter
よんぶんのいち
yonbun no ichi

A quarter of the pie is gone.

そのパイのよんぶんのいちがたべられています。

sono pai no yonbun no ichi ga taberareteimasu

queen
じょうおうさま jyooosama

She is queen of the zebras.

かのじょはシマウマたちのじょおうさまです。

kanojo wa shimauma-tachi no jyooosamadesu

question
しつもん shitsumon

She has a question.

かのじょはしつもんします。

kanojo wa shitsumon shimasu

quick
はやく hayaku

A rabbit is quick; a tortoise is slow.

うさぎははやく、かめはのろいです。

sagi wa hayaku kame wa noroi desu

quiet しずかな shizukana

Shh! Be quiet!

シー！しずかに！
shii! shizukani!

quilt
かけぶとん kakebuton

Who is under the quilt?

そのかけぶとんのしたにはだれがいますか？

sono kakebuton no shita niwa dare ga imasuka?

to quit やめる yameru

The raccoon wants to quit practicing.

そのアライグマはれんしゅうをやめようとおもっています。

sono araiguma wa renshyuu o yameyou to omotteimasu

quite まったく mattaku

It is quite cold today.

きょうはまったくさむい。
kyoo wa mattaku samui

Q

R

rabbit *See Animals (page 10).*
うさぎ usagi

race レース reesu

Who is going to win the race?

だれがレースにかつのでしょう?
dare ga reesu ni katsunodeshyoo?

radio
ラジオ radio

They listen to the radio.

かれらはラジオをききます。
karera wa radio o kikimasu

rain あめ ame

She likes the rain.

かのじょはあめがすきです。
kanojo wa ame ga sukidesu

rainbow
にじ niji

She is standing under a rainbow.

かのじょはにじのしたにたっています。
kanojo wa niji no shita ni tatte imasu

raincoat *See Clothing (page 24).*
レインコート rein-kooto

raindrop
あまだれ amadare

Look at the raindrops.

あまだれをみてごらん。
amadare o mite goran

rainy あめ ame

It's a rainy day.

あめのひだ。
ame no hi da

to read
よむ yomu

Does he know how to read?

かれはよみかたをしって
いますか?
kare wa yomikata o shitte
imasuka?

ready
しようとする shiyou to suru

The baby is not ready to go.

そのあかちゃんはゆこうとは
していません。
sono akachan wa yukoo towa
shiteimasen

real
ほんものの honmono no

It is not a real dog.

それはほんもののいぬではない。
sore wa honmono no inu dewa nai

really
ほんとうに hontooni.

She is really tall!

かのじょはほんとうにせがたかい!
kanojo wa hontooni se ga takai!

red *See Numbers and Colors (page 68).*
あか aka

refrigerator
れいぞうこ reizouko

We keep our snowballs in
the refrigerator.

わたしたちはそのれいぞうこの
なかにわたしたちのゆきのたま
をいれておきます。
watashitachi wa sono reizouko no
naka ni watashitachi no yuki no tama
o ireteokimasu

to remember
おもいだす omoidasu

It is hard to remember his
phone number.

かれのでんわばんごうをおもいだす
のはむずかしい。
kare no denwa bangoo o omoidasu
nowa muzukashii

restaurant
レストラン resutoran

She is eating at
a restaurant.

かのじょはレストランで
しょくじをしています。
kanojo wa resutoran de
shyokuji o shiteimasu

rice おこめ okome

Where is all the rice?

すべてのおこめはどこ
にいったの?
subete no okome wa doko
ni ittano?

rich
おかねもち
okanemochi

He is very rich.

かれはとてもおかねもちです。
kare wa totemo okanemochi desu

to ride
のる noru

It is fun to ride a horse.

うまにのるのはおもしろい。
uma ni noru nowa omoshiroi

right
みぎの migino

This is your right hand.

これはあなたのみぎてです。
kore wa anata no migi-te desu

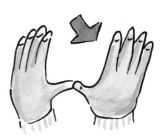

Rooms in a House
いえのなかのへや
ie no naka no heya

attic
やねうら
yaneura

deck
ベランダ
beranda

bedroom
しんしつ
shinshitsu

bathroom
ふろば
furoba

kitchen
キッチン
kittchin

dining room
ダイニングルーム
dainingu-ruum

garage
ガレージ
gareeji

playroom
ゆうぎしつ
yuugishitsu

closet
おしいれ
oshiire

bedroom
しんしつ
shinshitsu

office
オフィス
ofisu

living room
リビングルーム
libingu-ruumu

hall
ホール
hoolu

porch
げんかん
genkan

basement
ちかしつム
chikashitsu

laundry room
ランドリールーム
landorii-ruumu

ring
ゆびわ yubiwa

She has a new ring.

かのじょはあたらしいゆびわ
をしています。
kanojo wa atarashii yubiwa
o shiteimasu

to ring
なる naru

The telephone is
going to ring soon.

でんわがもうすぐなるでしょう。
denwa ga moosugu narudeshyoo

river
かわ kawa

I am floating down the river.

わたしはそのかわを
くだっています。
watashi wa sono kawa o
kudatte imasu

road
みち michi

The road goes over
the hill.

そのみちはそのおかを
こえます。
sono michi wa sono oka o
koemasu

robot
ロボット robotto

A robot is looking in
my window!

ひとつのロボットがわたしの
まどをのぞきこんでいます!
hitotsu no robotto ga watashi no
mado o nozokikonde imasu!

rock
いわ iwa

What is going around the rock?

そのいわのまわりではなに
がおきているのですか?
sono iwa no mawari dewa nani
ga okiteirunodesuka?

roof
やね yane

There is a cow on the roof.

そのやねのうえにめうし
がいっとういます。
sono yane no ue niwa meushi
ga ittoo imasu

room
へや heya

The little house has little rooms.

そのちいさないえにはちいさな
へやがあります。
sono chiisana ie niwa chiisana
heya ga arimasu

rooster *See Animals (page 10).*
オンドリ **ondori**

root
ねっこ **nekko**

The plant has deep roots.

そのしょくぶつにはふかい
ねっこがあります。
sono shyokubutsu niwa fukai
nekko ga arimasu

rose
バラ **bara**

She likes roses.

かのじょはバラがすきです。
kanojo wa bara ga sukidesu

round
まるい **marui**

These things are round.

これらのものはまるい。
korera no mono wa marui

to rub
さする **sasuru**

He is rubbing his tummy.

かれはじぶんのおなかを
さすっています。
kare wa jibun no onaka o
sasutte imasu

rug
しきもの **shikimono**

A bug is on the rug.

そのしきもののうえには
いっぴきのむしがいます。
sono shikimono no ue niwa
ippiki no mushi ga imasu

to run
はしる **hashiru**

You need feet to run!

あなたははしるためには
あしがひつようです！
anata wa hashiru tameniwa
ashi ga hituyoo desu!

running *See Games and Sports (page 44).*
ランニング **ranningu**

S

sad
かなしい kanashii

This is a sad face.

これはかなしいかおです。
kore wa kanashii kao desu

sailboat *See Transportation (page 108).*
ヨット yotto

salad
サラダ salada

He is making a salad.

かれはサラダをつくっています。
kare wa salada o tsukutte imasu

salt
しお shio

She is using too much salt.

かのじょはしおをふりかけすぎます。
kanojo wa shio o furikakesugimasu

same おなじ onaji

They look the same.

かれらはおなじようです。
karerawa onaji yoo desu

sand すな suna

There is a lot of sand at the beach.

そのはまべにはたくさんの
すながあります。
sono hamabe niwa takusan no
suna ga arimasu

sandwich
サンドウイッチ
sandouitch

It's a pickle sandwich! Yum!

それはつけもののサンドウイッチ
です! おいしそう!
sore wa tsukemono no sandouitch desu! oishisoo!

sandy
すながいっぱい
suna ga ippai

The beach is sandy.

そのはまべにはすなが
いっぱいあります。
sono hamabe niw suna ga ippai arimasu

Saturday
どようび doyoobi

On Saturday, we work together.

どようびにわたしたちは
いっしょにはたらきます。
doyoobi ni watashitachi wa issho ni hatarakimasu

sausage
ソーセージ sooseeji

This dog likes sausages.

このいぬはソーセージが
すきです。
kono inu wa sooseeji ga sukidesu

saw
のこぎり nokogiri

A saw is for cutting.

のこぎりはきるための
ものです。
nokogiri wa kiru tame no
mono desu

to say
いう iu

She wants to say hello.

かのじょはこんにちはと
いいたい。
kanojo wa konnichiwa to iitai

scarf *See Clothing (page 24).*
スカーフ sukaafu

school
がっこう gakkoo

He can learn in school.

かれはがっこうでべんきょう
できます。
kare wa gakkoo de benkyoo dekimasu

scissors
はさみ hasami

Look what he is cutting with
the scissors!

はさみでかれがなにを
きっているのかをみなさい!
hasami de kare ga nani o
kitteirunoka o minasai!

to scrub
ごしごしあらう
goshigoshi arau

He wants to scrub the tub.

かれはバスタブをごしごし
あらいたい。
kare wa basutabu o goshigoshi araitai

sea
うみ umi

Whales live in the sea.

くじらはうみにすんでいます。
kujira wa umi ni sunde imasu

seat
いす isu

The seat is too high.

そのいすはたかすぎる。
sono isu wa takasugiru

secret
ひみつ himitsu

She is telling him a secret.

かのじょはかれにひみつを
のべています。
kanojo wa kare ni himitsu o
nobete imasu

to see *See People (page 76).*
みる miru

seed たね tane

When you plant a seed, it grows.

あなたがたねをまくとせいちょうします。

anata ga tane o makuto seichoo shimasu

to sell うる uru

He sells balloons.

かれはふうせんをうります。

kare wa fuusen o urimasu

to send おくる okuru

Mom has to send a letter in the mail.

ママはゆうびんでてがみをおくらなければなりません。

mama wa yuubin de tegami o okuranakereba narimasen

September くがつ kugatsu

The month after August is September.

はちがつのつぎのつきはくがつです。

hachigatsu no tugi no tuki wa kugatsu desu

seven See Numbers and Colors (page 68).
しち shichi

seventeen See Numbers and Colors (page 68).
じゅうしち jyuushichi

seventy See Numbers and Colors (page 68).
しちじゅう shichijyuu

shark サメ same

A shark has many teeth.

サメにはたくさんのはがあります。

same niwa takusan no ha ga arimasu

shawl See Clothing (page 24).
ショール shoolu

she かのじょ kanojo

She is hiding.

かのじょはかくれています。

kanojo wa kakurete imasu

sheep See Animals (page 10).
ひつじ hitsuji

shirt See Clothing (page 24).
シャツ shyatsu

shoes See Clothing (page 24).
くつ kutsu

to shop
かいものをする
kaimono wo-suru

He likes to shop.

かれはかいものをするのがすきです。

kare wa kaimono o suru noga sukidesu

short
せがひくい se ga hikui

He is too short.

かれはせがひくすぎます。
kare wa se ge hikusugimasu

to shout
さけぶ sakebu

They have to shout.

かれらはさけばなければ
なりません。
karera wa sakebanakereba narimasen

shovel
シャベル shyabelu

She needs a bigger shovel.

かのじょはもっとおおきな
シャベルがひつようです。
kanojo wa motto ookina shyabelu ga hituyoo desu

show
ショー shoo

They are in a show.

かれらはショーをしています。
karera wa shoo o shiteimasu

to show
みせる miseru

Open wide to show your new tooth!

きみのあたらしいはをみせる
ためにくちをおおきくあけなさい。
kimi no atarashii ha o miseru tameni kuchi o ookiku akenasai

shy
はずかしがりや hazukashigariya

He is very shy.

かれはとてもはずかし
がりやです。
kare wa totemo hazukashigariya desu

sick
びょうきで byooki de

The poor rhinoceros is sick!

そのかわいそうなサイは
びょうきです!
sono kawaisoo na sai wa byooki desu!

side そばに soba-ni

The tree is on the side of the house.

そのきはそのいえのそばに
あります。
sono ki wa sono ie no soba ni arimasu

sidewalk
ほどう hodoo

They are playing on the sidewalk.

かれらはそのほどうで
あそんでいます。
karera wa sono hodoo de asonde imasu

sign
かんばん kanban

This is the bakery's sign.

これがそのぱんやさんの
かんばんです。
kore ga sono panya-san no kanban desu

silly
ばかげた bakageta

He has a silly smile.

かれはばかげたわらいをしています。
kare wa bakageta warai o shiteimasu

to sing
うたう utau

She loves to sing.

かのじょはうたうのがすきです。
kanojo wa utaunoga sukidesu

sister
おねえさん(いもうと)
oneesan(imooto)

They are sisters.

かのじょたちはきょうだいです。
kanojotachi wa kyoodai desu

to sit すわる suwaru

They want to sit.

かれらはすわりたい。
karera wa suwaritai

six *See Numbers and Colors (page 68).*
ろく roku

sixteen *See Numbers and Colors (page 68).*
じゅうろく jyuuroku

sixty *See Numbers and Colors (page 68).*
ろくじゅう rokujyuu

skateboard *See Transportation (page 108).*
スケートボード sukeeto-boodo

skates *See Transportation (page 108).*
スケート sukeeto

skating (ice) *See Games and Sports (page 44).*
(アイス)スケート aisu-sukeeto

skiing *See Games and Sports (page 44).*
スキー sukii

skirt *See Clothing (page 24).*
スカート sukaato

sky
そら sora

The sky is full of stars.

そらはほしたちでいっぱいです。
sora wa hoshi-tachi de ippaidesu

to sleep
ねる neuru

He is ready to sleep.

かれはねようとしています。
kare wa neyoo to shiteimasu

slow
のろい noroi

A rabbit is quick;
a tortoise is slow.

うさぎははやく、かめはのろい。
usagi wa hayaku, kame wa noroi

small
ちいさい chiisai

An ant is small.

ありはちいさい。
ari wa chiisai

to smell *See People (page 76).*
かぐ kagu

smile
ほほえみ hohoemi

What a big smile!

なんというおおきなほほえみだ!
nantoiu ookina hohoemi da!

smoke
けむり kemuri

Watch out for the smoke.

そのけむりにきをつけて
sono kemuri ni ki o tsukete

snail カタツムリ katatsumuri

He has a snail on his nose.

かれはじぶんのはなのうえに
カタツムリがいます。
kare wa jibun no hana no ue ni
katatsumui ga imasu

snake *See Animals (page 10).*
へび hebi

sneakers *See Clothing (page 24).*
スニーカー suniikaa

to snore
いびきをかく
ibiki o kaku

Try not to snore.

いびきをかかないように
しなさい。
ibiki wo kakanai yooni shinasai

snow
ゆき yuki

Snow is white and cold.

ゆきはしろくてつめたい。
yuki wa shirokute tsumetai

snowball
ゆきのたま yuki no tama

He is throwing snowballs.

かれはゆきのたまをなげています。
kare wa yuki no tama o nagete imasu

so
とても totemo

She is so tall!

かのじょはとてもせがたかい!
kanojo wa totemo se ga takai!

soap
せっけん sekken

He is using soap to wash.

かれはあらうためにせっけん
をつかっています。
kare wa arau tameni sekken
o tsukatte imasu

soccer *See Games and Sports (page 44).*
サッカー sakkaa

socks *See Clothing (page 24).*
ソックス sokkusu

sofa
ソファー sofaa

The zebras are sitting
on the sofa.

そのシマウマたちはソファー
のうえにすわっています。
sono shimauma-tachi wa sofaa
no ue ni suwatte imasu

some
なんびきか nanbikika

Some of them are pink.

かれらのうちなんびきかは
ピンクいろです。
karera no uchi nanbikika wa pinku-iro desu

someday
いつか itsuka

I can drive...
someday.

いつか... ぼくはうんてんできます。
itsuka... boku wa unten dekimasu

someone
だれか dareka

Someone is behind
the fence.

だれかがかきねのうしろ
にいます。
dareka ga kakine no ushiro
ni imasu

something
なにか nanika

Something is under the rug.

なにかがそのしきもの
のしたにいます。
nanika ga sono shikimono
no shita ni imasu

song
うた uta

A song is for singing.

うたはうたうためのものです。
uta wa utau tameno monodesu

soon
もうすぐ moosugu

Soon it is going to be noon.

もうすぐしょうごになります。
moosugu shoogo ni narimasu

sorry
ざんねん **zannen**

She is sorry she dropped it.

ざんねんなことにかのじょは
それをおとした。
zannen na koto ni kanojo wa
sore o otoshita

soup
スープ **suupu**

The soup is hot!

そのスープはあつい!
sono suupu wa atsui!

south
みなみ **minami**

It is warm in the south.

みなみではあたたかい。
minami dewa atatakai

special
とくしゅな **tokushu na**

This is a special car.

これはとくしゅなじどう
しゃです。
kore wa tokushu na jidoosha desu

spider
くも **kumo**

This spider is friendly.

このくもはしたしみやすい。
kono kumo wa shitashimi yasui

spoon
スプーン **supuun**

A spoon can't run, can it?

スプーンははしれませんね?
supuun wa hashiremasen ne?

spring
はる **haru**

Flowers grow in spring.

はなたちははるに
そだちます。
hana-tachi wa haru ni
sodachimasu

square
ましかく **mashikaku**

A square has four sides.

ましかくにはよっつのへんが
あります。
mashikaku niwa yottsu no hen ga arimasu

squirrel
リス **risu**

There is a squirrel on that hat.

そのぼうしのうえにはいっぴきの
リスがいます。
sono booshi no ue niwa ippiki no
risu ga imasu

stamp
きって **kitte**

A stamp goes on a letter.

てがみにはきってをはります。
tegami niwa kitte o harimasu

to stand
たつ tatsu

She does not like
to stand.

かのじょはたつのがすきでは
ありません。
kanojo wa tatsu noga sukidewa
arimasen

star
ほし hoshi

That star is winking.

そのほしはウインクしています。
sono hoshi wa uinku shiteimasu

to start
はじめる hajimeru

They want to start with A.

かれらはAからはじめたいです。
karera wa A kara hajimetai desu

to stay
いる iru

He has to stay inside.

かれはなかにいなければなりません。
kare wa naka ni inakereba narimasen

to step
ふむ fumu

Try not to step in the puddle.

みずたまりをふまないように
しなさい。
mizutamari o fumanai yooni shinasai

stick
ぼう boo

The dog wants the stick.

そのいぬはそのぼうがほしいです。
sono inu wa sono boo ga hoshii desu

sticky
ねばねばした
nebanebashita

That candy is sticky.

そのキャンデーはねばねば
しています。
sono kyandii ha nebaneba
shiteimasu

stomach *See People (page 76).*
い i

to stop
とまる tomaru

You have to stop for a
red light.

あなたはあかしんごうでは
とまらなければなりません。
anata wa aka-shingoo de wa tomaranakereba narimasen

store
みせ mise

She buys books at the store.

かのじょはそのみせでほん
をかいます。
kanojo wa sono mise de hon
o kaimasu

storm
あらし arashi

She does not like the storm.

かのじょはあらしがすきでは
ありません。
kanojo wa arashi ga sukidewa
arimasen

story
ものがたり monogatari

We all know this story.

わたしたちはみんなこの
ものがたりをしっています。
watashitachi wa minna kono
monogatari o shitte imasu

strange
きみょうな kimyoona

This is a strange animal.

これはきみょうなどうぶつです。
kore wa kimyoo na doobutsu desu

strawberry
いちご ichigo

This strawberry is big.

このいちごはおおきい。
kono ichigo wa ookii

street
とおり toori

There is an elephant in the street.

そのとおりにはぞうがいっぴき
います。
sono toori niwa zoo ga ippiki imasu

student
せいと seito

The students are all fish.

そのせいとたちはみんな
さかなです。
sono seito-tachi wa minna
sakanadesu

subway *See Transportation (page 108).*
ちかてつ chikatetsu

suddenly
とつぜん totsuzen

Suddenly, it is raining.

とつぜん、あめがふってきました。
totsuzen, ame ga futte kimashita

suit
スーツ suutsu

Something is spilling on
his suit.

なにかがかれのスーツにこ
ぼれています。
nanika ga kare no suutsu ni
koborete imasu

suitcase
スーツケース suutsukeesu

What is in that suitcase?

そのスーツケースのなかには
なにがありますか？
sono suutsukeesu no naka niwa
nani ga arimasuka?

summer なつ natsu

It is hot in summer.

なつはあつい。
natsu wa atsui

sun
たいよう taiyoo

The sun is hot.

たいようはあつい。
taiyoo wa atsui

Sunday
にちようび nichiyoobi

On Sunday, we eat dinner with Grandma.

にちようびに、わたしたち
はおばあちゃんとディナー
をたべます。
nichiyoobi ni, watashitachi
wa obaachan to dinaa o tabemasu

sunflower
ひまわり himawari

The sunflower is big and yellow.

そのひまわりはおおきくてきいろい。
sono himawari wa ookikute kiiroi

sunny
よくはれた yoku hareta

She loves sunny days.

かのじょはよくはれたひが
すきです。
kanojo wa yoku hareta hi ga sukidesu

sure
たしかな tashika na

I am sure the door is not going to open.

そのドアがひらこうとしない
のはたしかです。
sono doa ga hirakooo to shinai
nowa tashikadesu

surprised
びっくりして
bikkurishite

She is surprised.

かのじょはびっくりして
います。
kanojo wa bikkurishite imasu

sweater *See Clothing (page 24).*
セーター seetaa

to swim
およぐ oyogu

The fish likes to swim.

そのさかなはおよぐのが
すきです。
sono sakana wa oyogu noga
sukidesu

swimming *See Games and Sports (page 44).*
すいえい suiei

table テーブル **teebulu**

There is a chicken on the table.

そのテーブルのうえには
にわとりがいちわいます。
sono teebulu no ue niwa
niwatori ga ichiwa imasu

tail しっぽ **shippo**

He has a long tail.

かれはながいしっぽを
もっています。
kare wa nagai shippo o
motte imasu

to take もってゆく **motte yuku**

He is going to take the suitcase with him.

かれはそのスーツケースを
もってゆこうとしています。
kare wa sono suutsukesu o
motte yukoo to shite imasu

to talk はなす **hanasu**

They like to talk on the phone.

かれらはでんわではなす
のがすきです。
karera wa denwa de hanasu
noga sukidesu

tall せがたかい **se ga takai**

The red one is very tall.

そのあかいものはとてもせがたかい。
sono akai mono wa totemo
se ga takai

tambourine タンバリン **tanbarin**

Shake that tambourine!

そのタンバリンをふりなさい!
sono tanbarin o furinasai!

tan *See Numbers and Colors (page 68).*
ひやけのいろ **hiyake-no-iro**

to taste *See People (page 76).*
あじわう **ajiwau**

taxi *See Transportation (page 108).*
タクシー **takushii**

teacher せんせい **sensei**

Our teacher helps us to learn.

わたしたちのせんせいは
わたしたちがべんきょうする
のをてつだいます。
watashitachi no sensei wa
watashitachi ga benkyoo suru
nowo tetsudaimasu

tear なみだ **namida**

There is a tear on her cheek.

かれのほほにはなみだがあります。
kare no hoho niwa namida ga arimasu

telephone
でんわ denwa

People can call you on
the telephone.

ひとびとはあなたにでんわ
をかけられます。

hitobito wa anata ni denwa
o kakeraremasu

television
テレビ telebi

My goldfish likes to
watch television.

わたしのきんぎょは
テレビをみるのがすきです。

watashi no kingyo wa
telebi o mirunoga sukidesu

to tell
かたる kataru

Mom has to tell her the word.

ママはかのじょにそのことばを
かたらなければなりません。

mama wa kanojo ni sono kotoba
o kataranekereba narimasen

ten See Numbers and Colors (page 68).
じゅう jyuu

tennis See Games and Sports (page 44).
テニス tenisu

tent
テント tento

What is inside the tent?

そのテントのなかにはなに
がありますか?

sono tento no naka ni wa
nani ga arimasuka?

termite See Insects (page 52).
シロアリ shiroari

terrible
ひどい hidoi

What a terrible mess!

なんてひどいちらかしようだ!

nante hidoi chirakashi yoo da!

to thank
かんしゃする
kansha-suru

He wants to thank the
firefighter.

かれはそのしょうぼうし
さんにかんしゃしたい。

kare wa sono shoobooshi-san
ni kansha shitai

that それ sore

What is that?

それはなんですか?

sore wa nandesuka?

their
かれらの karera-no

They are pointing to their suitcases.

かれらはじぶんたちのスーツケースをゆびさしています。

karera wa jibuntachi no suutsukeesu o yubisashite imasu

these
これらの korerano

No one wants these eggs.

だれもこれらのたまごはほしくないです。

daremo korera no tamago wa hoshikunai desu

them
かれらに karera-ni

The shoes belong to them.

そのくつはかれらのものです。

sono kutsu wa karera no mono desu

they
かれら karera

See the mice?
They are dancing.

あのねずみたちがみえる?
かれらはおどっています。

ano nezumi-tachi ga mieru?
karera wa odotte imasu

then
それから sorekara

Get into bed. Then sleep.

ベッドにはいりなさい。
それからねむりなさい。

beddo ni hairinasai.
sorekara nemurinasai

thin
やせて yasete

One clown is thin.

ひとりのピエロはやせています。

hitori no piero wa yasete imasu

thing
もの mono

What is this thing?

このものはなんですか?
kono mono wa nandesuka?

there
あそこに asoko-ni

She's over there.

かのじょはあそこにいます。
kanojo wa asoko ni imasu

to think
かんがえる kangaeru

We use our brain to think.

わたしたちはかんがえるため
にあたまをつかいます。
watashitachi wa kangaeru tameni
atama o tsukaimasu

(to be) thirsty
のどがかわいて(いる)
nodo ga kawaite (iru)

He is thirsty.

かれはのどがかわいています。
kare wa nodo ga kawaite imasu

thirteen See Numbers and Colors (page 68).
じゅうさん jyuusan

thirty See Numbers and Colors (page 68).
さんじゅう sanjyuu

this
この kono

This baby is sad.

このあかちゃんはかなしい。
kono akachan wa kanashii

those
それらの sorera no

Those babies are happy.

それらのあかちゃんたちは
しあわせです。
sorera no akachan-tachi wa
shiawase desu

thousand See Numbers and Colors (page 68).
せん sen

three See Numbers and Colors (page 68).
さん san

through ぬけて nukete

The ball is coming through the window.

そのボールはそのまどを
つきぬけてはいってきています。
sono boolu wa sono mado o
tsukinukete haitte kite imasu

to throw
なげる nageru

We like to throw
the ball.

わたしたちはそのボール
をなげるのがすきです。
watashitachi wa sono boolu
o nagerunoga sukidesu

thumb See People (page 76).
おやゆび oya-yubi

thunder
かみなり kaminari

Thunder is loud.

かみなりはうるさい。
kaminari wa urusai

Thursday
もくようび **mokuyoobi**

On Thursday, we wash clothes.

もくようびにわたしたち
はふくをあらいます。
mokuyoobi ni watashitachi
wa fuku o araimasu

tie *See Clothing (page 24).*
ネクタイ **nekutai**

to tie
むすぶ **musubu**

Is he going to tie his shoelaces?

かれはじぶんのくつひもをむす
ぼうとしていますか?
kare wa jibun no kutsu-himo o
musububooto shite imasuka?

tiger
とら **tora**

This is a tiger.

これはいっぴきのとらです。
kore wa ippiki no tora desu

time
とき **toki**

It is time to wash the dishes.

おさらをあらうときです。
osara o arau toki desu

tire
タイヤ **taiya**

The tire is flat.

そのタイヤはパンクしています。
sono taiya wa panku shite imasu

tired
つかれて **tsukarete**

She is tired.

かのじょはつかれています。
kanojo wa tsukarete imasu

to へ **e**

He is going to school.

かれはがっこうへいっています。
kare wa gakko e itte imasu

today
きょう **kyoo**

Today is her birthday.

きょはかのじょのたんじょ
うびです。
kyoo wa kanojo no tanjoobi desu

toe *See People (page 76).*
つまさき **tsumasaki**

together
いっしょに isshoni

They are sitting together.

かれらはいっしょにすわっ
ています。
karera wa issho ni suwatte
imasu

tomato
トマト tomato

Mmm! It is a big,
juicy tomato.

おいしそう!それはひとつのおおき
くてみずみずしいトマトです。
oishisoo! sore wa hitotsu no ookikute
mizumizushii tomato desu

tomorrow
あした ashita

Tomorrow is another day.

あしたはべつのひです。
ashita wa betsu no hi desu

tonight
こんや konya

He is sleepy tonight.

かれはこんやはねむたい。
kare wa konya wa nemutai

too
も mo

The baby is singing, too.

そのあかちゃんもな
いています。
sono akachan mo naite imasu

tooth *See People (page 76).*
は ha

toothbrush
はぶらし haburashi

My toothbrush is red.

わたしのはぶらしはあかいろです。
watashi no haburashi wa aka-iro desu

top
てっぺん teppen

The bird is on top.

そのとりはてっぺんにいます。
sono tori wa teppen ni imasu

to touch *See People (page 76).*
さわる sawaru

towel
タオル taolu

He needs a towel.

かれにはいちまいのタオ
ルがひつようです。
kare niwa ichimai no taolu
ga hitsuyoo desu

town
まち machi

The ant lives in a town.

そのアリはひとつのまちに
すんでいます。
sono ari wa hitotsu no machi
ni sunde imasu

toy
おもちゃ omocha

He has all kinds
of toys.

かれはすべてのしゅるいの
おもちゃをもっています。
kare wa subete no syurui no
omocha o motte imasu

track
あしあと ashiato

That is a rabbit track.

それはいっぴきのうさぎの
あしあとです。
sore wa ippiki no usagi no
ashiato desu

train *See Transportation (page 108).*
でんしゃ densha

treat
ごちそう gochisoo

A bone is a treat.

ほねはごちそうです。
hone wa gochisoo desu

tree
き ki

There is a cow in that tree.

あのきのうえにいっとうの
めうしがいます。
ano ki no ue ni ittoo no
meushi ga imasu

triangle
さんかく sankaku

A triangle has
three sides.

さんかくにはみっつの
へんがあります。
sankaku niwa mittsu no
hen ga arimasu

(to do) tricks
まほう(をする)
mahoo (o-suru)

Her job is to do tricks.

かれのしごとはまほうをす
ることです。
kare no shigoto wa mahoo
o surukoto desu

trip
りょこう ryokoo

She is going on a trip.

かのじょはりょこう
にでかけます。
kanojo wa ryokoo ni dekakemasu

to trip
ころぶ korobu

It is not fun to trip.

ころぶのはたのしくありません。
korobu nowa tanoshiku arimasen

Transportation
こうつう
kootsuu

airplane
ひこうき
hikooki

train
でんしゃ
densha

van
バン
ban

skateboard
スケートボード
sukeeto-boodo

bicycle
じてんしゃ
jitensha

skates
スケート
sukeeto

helicopter
ヘリコプター
helikoputaa

sailboat
ヨット
yotto

car
じどうしゃ
jidoosha

truck
トラック
torakku

boat
ボート
booto

subway
ちかてつ
chikatetsu

horse
うま
uma

taxi
タクシー
takushii

bus
バス
basu

109

truck *See Transportation (page 108).*
トラック torakku

trumpet
トランペット **toranpetto**

This is a trumpet.

これはいっこのトランペットです。
kore wa ikko no toranpetto desu

to try
しようとする
shiyou-to-suru

He tries to climb.

かれはのぼろうとします。
kare wa noboroo to shimasu

Tuesday
かようび **kayoobi**

On Tuesday we wash the floors.

かようびにわたしたち
はゆかをあらいます。
kayoobi ni watashitachi
wa yuka o araimasu

tulip
チューリップ **chyuurippu**

There is a tulip on his head.

かれのあたまのうえにはいっぽん
のチューリップがあります。
kare no atama no ue niwa ippon
no chyuurippu ga arimasu

to turn
まわす **mawasu**

You have to turn it.

あなたはそれをまわさ
なければなりません。
anatawa sore o
mawasanakereba narimasen

turtle
かめ **kame**

That is a fast turtle!

それはとてもはやい
かめです!
sore wa totemo hayai
kame desu!

twelve *See Numbers and Colors (page 68).*
じゅうに **jyuuni**

twenty *See Numbers and Colors (page 68).*
にじゅう **nijyuu**

twins
ふたご **futago**

They are twins.

かれらはふたごです。
karera wa futago desu

two *See Numbers and Colors (page 68).*
に **ni**

ugly
みにくい minikui

Do you think the toad is ugly?

あなたはあのヒキガエルがみ
にくいとおもいますか?
anatawa ano hikigaeru ga
minikui to omoimasuka?

umbrella
かさ kasa

She has a yellow umbrella.

かのじょはいっぽんのきいろい
かさをもっています。
kanojo wa ippon no kiiroi kasa o
motte imasu

uncle おじさん ojisan

My uncle is my dad's brother.

ぼくのおじさんはぼくのパパの
おにいさんです。
boku no ojisan wa boku no papa
no oniisan desu

under
したに shita-ni

There is something
under the bed.

そのベッドのしたにはな
にかがある。
ono beddo no shita niwa
nanika ga aru

until まで made

He eats until he is full.

かれはおなかがいっぱいになる
までたべます。
kare wa onaka ga ippai ni
narumade tabemasu

up
うえでは ue-dewa

It's scary up here!

このうえではこわい!
kono ue dewa kowai!

upon
うえに ue-ni

The box is upon the box,
upon the box.

そのはこは、はことはこの
うえにあります。
sono hako wa hako to hako
no ue ni arimasu

upside-down
さかさまに sakasama ni

He is upside-down.

かれはさかだちしています。
kare wa sakadachi shiteimasu

us
わたしたちと
watashitachi to

Come with us!

わたしたちといっしょ
にきなさい!
watashitachi to issho ni kinasai!

to use つかう tsukau

He needs to use a comb.

かれはいっぽんのくしをつか
うことがひつようです。
kare wa ippon no kushi o tukau
koto ga hituyoo desu

V

vacation
きゅうか kyuuka

They are on vacation.

かれらはきゅうかちゅうです。
karera wa kyuuka chyuu desu

vacuum cleaner
でんきそうじき denki-soojiki

And here is the vacuum cleaner!

そしてここにでんきそうじきが
あります！
soshite koko ni denki-soojiki ga arimasu!

van *See Transportation (page 108).*
バン ban

vegetable
やさい yasai

He likes vegetables.

かれはやさいがすきです。
kare wa yasai ga sukidesu

very とても totemo

It is very cold in there.

そこはとてもさむいです。
soko wa totemo samuidesu

vest *See Clothing (page 24).*
ベスト besuto

veterinarian
じゅういさん jyuui-san

A veterinarian helps
animals.

じゅういさんはどうぶつ
たちをたすけます。
jyuui-san wa doobutsu-tachi
o tasukemasu

village
むら mura

What a pretty village!

なんてきれいなむらだ！
nante kireina mura da!

violin
バイオリン baiolin

He is playing the violin.

かれはバイオリンをひ
いています。
kare wa baiolin o hiite imasu

to visit
たずねる tazuneru

He is going to visit
Grandma.

かれはおばあちゃんをたず
ねています。
kare wa obaachan o tazunete imasu

volcano
かざん kazan

Don't go near the volcano!

そのかざんのちかくにはい
かないように！
sono kazan no chikaku niwa
ikanai yoo ni!

to wait
まつ matsu

He is waiting for a bus.

かれはバスをまっています。
kare wa basu o matte imasu

to wake up
めをさます me-o-samasu

He is about to wake up.

かれはめをさまそうとし
ています。
kare wa me o samsoo to
shiteimasu

to walk
あるく aruku

It is good to walk.

あるくのはよいことです。
arukunowa yoikoto desu

wall
かべ kabe

John is building a wall.

ジョンはひとつのかべを
つくっています。
Jon wa hitotsu no kabe o
tsukutte imasu

warm
あたたかい atatakai

It is warm by the fire.

ひのそばはあたたかい。
hi no soba wa atatakai

to wash
あらう arau

It takes a long time to
wash some things.

あるものをあらうのには
じかんがかかります。
aru mono o arau niwa
jikan ga kakarimasu

wasp *See Insects (page 52).*
カリバチ karibachi

watch
うでどけい ude-dokei

Robert is wearing his new
watch.

ロバートはかれのあたらしい
うでどけいをつけています。
Robaato wa kare no atarashii
ude-dokei o tukete imasu

to watch
みる miru

Peter likes to watch ants.

ピーターはアリたちをみる
のがすきです。
Piitaa wa ari-tachi o mirunoga
sukidesu

water
みず mizu

The pool is full of water.

そのプールはみずで
いっぱいです。
sono puulu wa mizu de ippai desu

we
わたしたち watashitachi

See us? We are all purple.

わかりますか?わたしたちはみん
なむらさきいろです。
wakarimasuka? watashitachi wa
minna murasaki-iro desu

weather
てんき tenki

What is the weather like today?

きょうのてんきはなんですか?
kyoo no tenki wa nandesuka?

Wednesday
すいようび suiyoobi

On Wednesday, we go to work.

すいようびに、わたしたちはは
たらきにゆきます。
suiyoobi ni watashitachi wa
hataraki ni yukimasu

week しゅう syuu

Seven days make a week.

いっしゅうかんはなのかです。
issyuukan wa nanoka desu

welcome
かんげいされる

kangei-sareru

We are always welcome at
Grandma's house.

わたしたちはおばあちゃん
のいえではいつもかんげ
いされます。
watashitachi wa obaachan no
ie dewa itsumo kangei saremasu

well
じょうずに jyoozu-ni

Thomas builds very well.

トーマスはとてもじょうずに
つくります。
toomasu wa totemo jyoozu ni
tsukurimasu

well
げんきで genki-de

She is not well.

かのじょはげんきではありません。
kanojo wa genki dewa arimasen

west
にし nishi

The sun goes down in the west.

たいようはにしにしずみます。
taiyoo wa nishi ni shizumimasu

wet ぬれて nurete

William is wet.

ウイリアムはぬれています。
uiliamu wa nurete imasu

what
なに nani

What is outside the window?

そのまどのそとにはなにが
ありますか?

sono mado no soto niwa nani ga
arimasuka?

wheel
しゃりん sharin

The bicycle needs a
new wheel.

そのじてんしゃはあたらしいし
ゃりんがひとつひつようです。

sono jitensha wa atarashii sharin
ga hitotsu hitsuyoo desu

when
とき toki

When you sleep, you close
your eyes.

あなたがねむるとき、
あなたはめをとじます。

anataga nemuru toki, anata
wa me o tojimasu

where
ばしょ basho

This is where he keeps
his dinner.

ここがかれがじぶんのディナー
をいれているばしょです。

koko ga kare ga jibun no dinaa
o ireteiru basho desu

which
どちら dochira

Which one do you want?

あなたはどちらがほしいですか?

anata wa dochira ga hoshii desuka?

while
あいだに aida-ni

I run while he sleeps.

わたしはかれがねむっている
あいだにはしります。

watashi wa kare ga nemutteiru
aida ni hashirimasu

whiskers
ひげ hige

This animal has long whiskers.

このどうぶつはながいひげ
をもっています。

kono doobutsu wa nagai hige o
motte imasu

to whisper
ささやく sasayaku

This animal needs to whisper.

このどうぶつはささやく
のがひつようです。

kono doobutsu wa sasayaku
noga hitsuyoo desu

whistle ふえ fue

They can hear the whistle.

かれらはそのふえをきく
ことができます。

arera wa sono fue o kikukoto
ga dekimasu

white *See Numbers and Colors (page 68).*
しろ shiro

who だれ dare

Who are you?

あなたはだれですか?

anata wa daredesuka?

whole
ぜんぶ zenbu

Can she eat the whole thing?

かのじょはぜんぶをた
べきれますか?
kanojo wa zenbu
o tabekiremasuka?

why
なぜ naze

Why is the baby crying?

なぜそのあかちゃんはない
ているのですか?
naze sono akachan wa naite
iru nodesuka?

wife
つま tsuma

She is his wife.

かのじょはかれのつまです。
kanojo wa kare no tsuma desu

wind
かぜ kaze

The wind is blowing.

かぜがふいています。
kaze ga fuite imasu

window
まど mado

I can see through the window.

わたしはまどごしにみえます。
watashi wa madogoshi ni miemasu

to wink
ウインクする
uinku-suru

It is fun to wink.

ウインクするのはたのしい。
uinku suru nowa tanoshii

winter
ふゆ fuyu

He skis in the winter.

かれはふゆにスキーをします。
kare wa fuyu ni sukii o shimasu

wish
ねがいごと negai-goto

The girl has a wish.

かのじょはねがいごと
をもっています。
kanojo wa negai-goto o
motte imasu

with
いっしょに issho-ni

The cat is dancing with
the dog.

そのねこはそのいぬといっ
しょにおどっています。
sono neko wa sono inu to issho ni odotte imasu

without
いっしょではなく
issho dewa naku

He is going without his sister.

かれはおねえさんといっしょでは
なくゆきます。
kare wa oneesan to issho dewa naku yukimasu

woman
じょせい josei

My grandmother is a nice woman.

わたしのおばあさんはすてきな
じょせいです。
watashi no obaasan wa sutekina josei desu

wonderful
すばらしい subarashii

They are wonderful dancers.

かれらはすばらしい
ダンサーたちです。
karera wa subarashii
dansaa-tachi desu

woods
もり mori

Someone is walking in the woods.

だれかがもりのなかをあるいています。
dareka ga mori no naka o aruite imasu

word
ことば kotoba

Do not say a word.

ひとこともいってはいけません。
hitokoto mo itte wa ikemasen

work
しごと shigoto

That is hard work.

それはきついしごとです。
sore wa kitsui shigoto desu

to work
はたらく hataraku

She has to work hard today.

かのじょはきょうはとても
はたらかなければなりません。
kanojo wa kyoo wa totemo hatarakanakereba narimasen

world
せかい sekai

The world is beautiful.

せかいはうつくしい。
sekai wa utsukushii

worried
こまった komatta

He looks worried.

かれはこまっているようです。
kare wa komatte iru yoo desu

to write
かく kaku

Katherine is trying to write with the pencil.

キャサリンはそのえんぴつで
かこうとしています。
Kyasarin wa sono enpitsu de kakoo to shiteimasu

wrong
まちがった machigatta

They are putting on the wrong hats.

かれらはまちがったぼうし
をかぶっています。
karera wa machigatta booshi o kabutte imasu

X

X-ray
レントゲン rentogen

The X-ray shows his bones.

そのレントゲンはかれのほねをみせます。
sono rentogen wa kare no hone o misemasu

xylophone
もっきん mokkin

He is a great xylophone player.

かれはすぐれたもっきんの
えんそうしゃです。
kare wa sugureta mokkin no
ensoosha desu

Y

yard
にわ niwa

There is a dinosaur
in our yard.

わたしたちのにわにきょうりゅ
うがいっぴきいます。
watashitachi no niwa ni kyooryuu
ga ippiki imasu

yawn
あくび akubi

What a big yawn!

なんておおきなあくびだ!
nante ookina akubi da!

year
ねん nen

He runs all year.

かれはねんじゅうはしります。
kare wa nenjyuu hashirimasu

yellow *See Numbers and Colors (page 68).*
きいろ kiiro

yes
はい hai

Is he yellow? Yes! He is.

かれはきいろいですか?はい!
かれはきいろいです。
kare wa kiiroi desuka? hai! kare wa kiiroidesu

yesterday
きのう kinoo

Yesterday is the day
before today.

きのはきょうのまえのひです。
kinoo wa kyoo no mae no hi desu

you
あなた anata

You are reading this book.

あなたはこのほんをよんでいます。
anata wa kono hon o yondeimasu

your
あなたの anata-no

What color are your eyes?

あなたのめのいろはなんですか?
anata no me no iro wa nandesuka?

zebra
シマウマ shimauma

You cannot have a pet zebra!

あなたはペットのシマウマをも
つことはできません!
anata wa petto no shimauma o
motsukoto wa dekimasen!

zero *See Numbers and Colors (page 68).*
ぜろ zero

zigzag
ジグザグもよう
jiguzagu-moyoo

The house has zigzags on it.

そのいえはジグザグもようです。
sono ie wa jiguzagu moyoo desu

to zip
ジッパーをあげる
jippaa o ageru

The bee wants to zip her jacket.

そのはちはかのじょのジャケット
のジッパーをあげたいです。
sono hachi wa kanojo no jaketto no
jippaa o agetaidesu

zipper
ジッパー jippaa

The zipper is stuck.

そのジッパーはうごきません。
sono jippaa wa ugokimasen

zoo
どうぶつえん
doobutsuen

I can see many animals
at the zoo.

わたしはそのどうぶつえん
ではたくさんのどうぶつを
みることができます。
watashi wa sono doobutsuen
dewa takusan no doobutsu o
mirukoto ga dekimasu

to zoom
きゅうにあがる
kyuu ni agaru

A rocket seems to zoom into space.

ひとつのロケットがうちゅう
にむけてきゅうにあがって
いるようです。
hitotsu no roketto ga
uchyuu ni mukete
kyuu ni agatteiru
yoo desu

A Family Dinner
かぞくのディナー
kazoku no dinaa

**Dinner is ready!
It's time to eat.**
ばんごはんができました!
たべるときです。
bangohan ga dekimashita!
taberu toki desu

**The chicken and vegetables
look delicious.**
にわとりとやさいは
おいしそうです。
niwatori to yasai wa
oishisoo desu

Here is your napkin.
ほらあなたの
ナプキンですよ。
hora anata no
napukin desuyo

Mmmm! They *are* delicious!
おいしそう! それらはおいしい!
oishisoo! sorera wa oishii!

**Please, can you pass
the salt and pepper?**
どうか、しおとこしょう
をまわしてください。
dooka, shio to koshoo o mawashite kudasai

Dinner is great.
Thanks, Mom.
ばんごはんはすてきです。
ありがとう、ママ。
bangohan wa suteki desu.
arigatoo, mama

You're welcome, dear.
どういたしまして。
dooitasihmashite

Do you want
more milk?
もっとミルクがほしい
ですか?
motto miluku ga hoshii
desuka?

No, thank you.
いいえ、いりません。
iie, irimasen

May I please be excused?
ちょっとせきをはずして
よいですか?
chotto seki o hazushite yoidesuka?

In a few minutes!
But please help us clear
the table first.
ちょっとあとで!
でもまずテーブルをきれい
にするのをてつだって。
chotto ato de!
demo mazu teebulu o kirei
ni suruno o tetsudatte

Of course.
もちろんです。
mochiron desu

Meeting and Greeting
であいとあいさつ
deai to aisatsu

Hello!
こんにちは!
konnichiwa!

Hi!
こんにちは!
konnichiwa!

How are you?
げんきですか?
genki desuka?

I am fine, thank you.
わたしはげんきです。
ありがとう。
watashi wa genki desu. aigatoo.

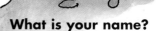

What is your name?
あなたのなまえはなんといいますか?
anata no namae wa nan to iimasuka?

My name is Maria.
What is your name?
わたしのなまえはマリアです。
あなたのなまえはなんといいますか?
anata no namae wa nan to iimasuka?

My name is Susan.
わたしのなまえはスーザンです。
watashi no namae wa Suuzan desu

What a beautiful day!
なんてすてきなひ!
nante sutekina hi!

Do you live near the park?
あなたはこうえんのちかく
にすんでいますか?
anata wa kooen no chikaku ni sunde imasuka?

Yes, I live across the street.
はい、わたしはとおりのむこう
にすんでいます。
hai, watashi wa toori no mukoo ni sundeimasu

Where do you live?
あなたはどこにすんでいますか?
anata wa doko ni sunde imasuka?

I live on Main Street.
わたしはめぬきどおりにすんで
います。
watashi wa menuki doori ni sunde imasu

Do you know what time it is?
いまなんじかわかりますか?
ima nanji ka wakarimasuka?

It is three o'clock.
さんじです。
sanji desu

Oh, I have to go now.
ああ、わたしはもうゆかなければなりません。
aa, watashi wa moo yukanakereba narimasen

It was nice to meet you.
おあいできてうれし
かったです。
oai dekite ureshikatta desu

Good-bye!
さようなら!
sayoonara!

See you soon.
またあいましょう。
mata aimashoo

Word List

A

a/an, 7
across, 7
add, 7
adventure, 7
aeroplane, 108
afraid, 7
after, 7
again, 7
agree, 7
air, 7
airport, 8
all, 8
alligator, 10
almost, 8
along, 8
already, 8
and, 8
answer, 8
ant, 53
apple, 9
April, 9
arm, 76
armadillo, 9
around, 9
art, 9
as, 9
ask, 12
at, 12
attic, 86
August, 12
aunt, 12
autumn, 12
awake, 12
away, 12

B

baby, 13
back, 13
backyard, 13
bad, 13
bag, 13
bakery, 13
ball, 13
balloon, 13

banana, 13
band, 13
bandage, 14
bank, 14
bark, 14
baseball, 44
basement, 87
basket, 14
basketball, 44
bat, 14
bat, 14
bath, 14
bathroom, 86
be, 14
beach, 15
beans, 15
bear, 10
beautiful, 15
because, 15
bed, 15
bedroom, 86
bee, 53
beetle, 52
before, 15
begin, 15
behind, 16
believe, 16
bell, 16
belt, 24
berry, 16
best, 16
better, 16
between, 16
bicycle, 108
big, 16
bird, 17
birthday, 17
biscuit, 17
black, 69
blank, 17
blanket, 17
blouse, 25
blow, 17
blue, 69
boat, 109
book, 17
bookshop, 17
boots, 25
bottle, 18

bowl, 18
bowling, 44
box, 18
boy, 18
branch, 18
brave, 18
bread, 18
break, 18
breakfast, 18
bridge, 19
bring, 19
broom, 19
brother, 19
brown, 69
brush, 19
bubble, 19
bug, 19
build, 19
bus, 109
bush, 20
busy, 20
but, 20
butter, 20
butterfly, 52
button, 20
buy, 20
by, 20

C

cage, 21
cake, 21
call, 21
camel, 21
camera, 21
can, 21
candle, 21
cap, 24
car, 109
card, 22
cardigan, 25
care, 22
carpenter, 22
carrot, 22
carry, 22
castanet, 22
castle, 22

cat, 22
caterpillar, 53
catch, 23
cave, 23
celebrate, 23
chair, 23
chalk, 23
change, 23
cheer, 23
cheese, 23
cherry, 26
child, 26
chocolate, 26
circle, 26
circus, 26
city, 26
clap, 26
class, 26
classroom, 27
clean, 27
climb, 27
clock, 27
close, 27
cloud, 27
clown, 28
coat, 25
cock, 11
cold, 28
comb, 28
come, 28
computer, 28
cook, 28
count, 28
country, 29
cow, 11
crayon, 29
cricket, 53
crowded, 29
cry, 29
cup, 29
cupboard, 87
cut, 29
cute, 29
cycling, 45